Life, Faith,
and Saltwater Taffy

Life, Faith,
and Saltwater Taffy

J.B. Hazelton

Illustrations by Jenny Shute

RESOURCE *Publications* · Eugene, Oregon

Resource Publications
An Imprint of Wipf and Stock Publishers
199 W. 8th Ave., Suite 3
Eugene, OR 97401

www.wipfandstock.com

PAPERBACK ISBN: 978-1-6667-1634-4
HARDCOVER ISBN: 978-1-6667-1635-1
EBOOK ISBN: 978-1-6667-1636-8

JANUARY 10, 2022 2:26 PM

CONTENTS

PREFACE

IN THE WINTER OF 2009, three friends came from different states and met for a memorable trip down the Florida Keys. We are close in age and chose to celebrate a big birthday together. We knew the vacation would be a rare treat, perhaps even a once-in-a-lifetime trip. We didn't realize it would be life-changing.

In Florida, we soaked in the warm sun and joked about how the snow and ice of a Midwest winter were melting off my friends, Jan and Kathy, while I was drying out from the cold rain of the Northwest. We gazed in awe at the sparkling turquoise water surrounding us, and marveled at the wonders of its depths from aboard a glass-bottom boat. We met dolphins in the sea and little Key deer on the land. We relaxed by the pool while steel drums serenaded us. As we talked about our dreams and our struggles, I shared my dream of writing; never imagining the trip itself would start a chain of events which would lead to writing this book.

As the vacation came to an end and we prepared to go our separate ways, we agreed that the time together, away from our daily routines, had made a significant impact on our lives. We even wondered if there was some way for us to enable others to have a similar experience. Over coffee in the Miami airport, we discussed the idea of offering retreats in a ministry context. With the beauty of the Keys fresh in our minds, we considered a beach theme. All three of us love the beach and also knew there was rich symbolism in the cleansing, refreshing, life-giving water. As a fundamental part of creation, water has much to teach about the Creator.

Over the next few months, my friend, Jan, and I sensed a call and began Beach Walk Ministries. Kathy chose a behind-the-scenes role and has continued to bless us with her encouragement and prayers.

We discussed various retreat topics and searched for a way to organize them. In a flash of inspiration, the idea of *the beach bag* came to me. When we head to the beach, what we do or do not bring along can determine how much we enjoy the experience, and our preparedness for whatever we might encounter. Isn't it also true that what we carry through life profoundly affects each day? What if we used items we take to the beach to represent aspects of our lives? As this concept grabbed my imagination, I gathered an abundance of ideas and Scripture verses. Soon Jan pointed out I was heading into deep waters, beyond what could be covered at a retreat. She quipped that I had enough material to write a book. I *think* she was joking, but the idea had been spoken into being.

The beach theme has resonated with retreat participants, enabling us to share both meaningful discussions and much laughter. Now, writing this book is giving me the opportunity to invite readers to join me as we explore these ideas, and their application, in greater depth.

Acknowledgments

THANKS TO MY FATHER, who passed along a love of language, a love of the water, and the DNA of the children of Israel.

To my mother—Thank you for filling our home with music and art. As a child, if I left you a note before going out, I would return to find the spelling and grammar had been corrected. I guess you were my first editor!

Jan "Falph" Abrahamson-Liscom, my dear friend and co-founder of Beach Walk Ministries—Your offhand remark first sparked the idea for writing this book, and your support and feedback have been invaluable ever since.

My husband, Jeff—Your unwavering support of this project helped me persist.

Gloria Campbell and Maryann West—I have learned so much from you!

Barb, Sue, and Mike—You're my writing tribe! Thanks for the encouragement, the suggestions, and the laughter.

Kathy S.—You've been like a sister since our New York days. Thanks for cheering me on.

Jenny—Collaborating with you has been a joy, and your artistry has added much to this book.

Shana, Kathy V., and my mother, as well as all who participated in a writing group with me—Thanks for your patience as I began putting ideas into words.

Everyone at Wipf and Stock Publishers—Thank you for taking this dream to the finish line.

NOTE TO READER

PERSPECTIVE CAN BE FOUND in the sharing of our thoughts, and healing can be found in the sharing of our stories. It is my hope and prayer that as you read about the joys, struggles, and insights that are part of my life path, you will find encouragement for yours. I hope you will have the opportunity to share part of your story with others, too. The "Diving Deeper" section at the end of each chapter is designed for discussion with a friend or a small group, as well as to enrich your own reading experience.

Before we spend more time together, let me introduce myself. Like many of you, I am a parent and a child, a spouse and a friend. Having grown up on the East Coast, and now living on the West Coast, I have an abiding love for the water. With a Master's in Music Education and a minor in Religion, I enjoy playing and teaching music, and working as a church musician. Like most of you, my life has been full of countless blessings, as well as times of uncertainty and pain.

My faith developed within a unique family background. On one side, my grandparents were Norwegian-American: a Lutheran pastor/seminary professor and a church organist. On the other side, they were Jewish immigrants from Germany and Russia. I wear cozy Norwegian sweaters—and love the show *Fiddler on the Roof.*

After my parents divorced and each remarried, a Roman Catholic stepfamily was added to the mix, and I gained a priest for a stepbrother. The family tree includes a Russian Orthodox priest, as well. The disparate beliefs and attitudes within my family have occasionally presented challenges, but they have also stirred consideration of my own beliefs. My learning has continued through countless Bible studies, Hebrew classes, and a study-tour of the Holy Land.

Over the years I have worked for, worshiped with, and learned from, a wide variety of faith communities within the Judeo-Christian tradition. I have come to appreciate what each has to offer. While I do not believe any human being or group can have perfect understanding of an infinite God and all the right answers, we grow when we wrestle with the right questions. Perhaps this book will raise a few!

Finally, I believe the Scriptures are a storehouse of wisdom for living, available to all. So, whatever your background or beliefs, welcome, and may you find inspiration within these pages.

Part I

To the Beach

Chapter 1

WATER

I must go down to the seas again, to the lonely sea and the sky
And all I ask is a tall ship and a star to steer her by

JOHN MASEFIELD, *SEA FEVER, SALT-WATER BALLADS*

IMAGINE YOURSELF AT THE beach. Which soundtrack would you choose? Would it be carefree Beach Boys music, or the wistful melody of "Shenandoah"? Would you choose the ominous theme from *Jaws*? If so, the ocean may not be your favorite place! There are many types of beaches. For different people, different images may come to mind. Regardless of whether a beach touches a quiet lake, a flowing river, or the restless sea, one thing is for sure—it's not a beach without water.

Now picture your favorite place outdoors. It could be a beach, or it could be a garden, a field of wheat, a desert, a forest, or the top of a mountain. Imagine you are there. Breathe deeply. What does the air smell like? Feel the warm sun or the chilly wind. Now, in your mind's eye, look around. If you are picturing a forest or mountain, do you see snow, an alpine lake, or a stream? If you're picturing a garden or a field, think of how rain nurtures the plants. If your happy place is the desert, water will be harder to find, but it is there, and it is essential.

Life cannot exist without water. Our bodies consist of more water than anything else, and our brains are 80 percent water. Scientists have even found that the mineral content of our blood plasma is very similar to seawater.

Water, in all its varied forms, sustains our physical being, enriches the soul, and speaks powerfully to the heart. What scene could be more carefree than a child flying a kite at the beach on a sunny day? But water can also be frightening. Imagine being on a ship, out of sight of land, tossed about in a fierce storm.

Each of us has had different experiences with water over our lifetime. Those reading this book with a friend or a group will have a chance to share stories, and if we were sitting face to face, I would love to hear yours. Let me share mine:

In many ways, water has defined my life. I like to think my first cry at birth was because I didn't want to leave my personal prenatal swimming pool. As a young child, I took swim lessons. At the end of one session, we had a race. The whistle blew; I closed my eyes against the chlorinated water and swam as fast as I could . . . diagonally across the pool. That was the beginning—and the end—of my competitive swimming career! However, I continued to enjoy swimming. Unlike running or walking, there was a certain relaxed pace at which I felt I could go on forever.

As a child living on Long Island, New York, I loved being on our family's cabin cruiser. Some nights we'd just head down to the boat for dinner, picking up a pizza near the marina. Family vacations often meant cruising on Long Island Sound and I loved being rocked to sleep at night by the gentle waves. I also learned to sail, and delighted in listening to every splash and gurgle of the water while partnering with the wind to travel from place to place.

My father, who was middle-aged by the time I was born, had served in the Navy during World War II. Despite some hair-raising experiences as a gunnery officer on a destroyer in the north Atlantic, he still loved the sea. I often heard him quote John Masefield's poem "Sea Fever." When I was asked to memorize a poem as a homework assignment, I immediately chose that one. I later learned that the expression "tall ship," meaning a sailboat with tall masts, originated with this poem.

When our family took a vacation by car, our usual destination was New Hampshire, where my father was raised. We headed straight for the Lakes Region and stayed in a cabin on the shore of a charming lake. I always looked forward to water-skiing in the afternoon, however my fondest memories are of the times my father and I swam in the lake. Dad was a lawyer who often seemed preoccupied with his work, even on vacations. However, when he and I swam out to a small island, he was fully present and we enjoyed each other's company. Those are memories I treasure.

My mother, despite her North Dakota upbringing, also loves all things nautical. When my family would go to Jones Beach on the South Shore of Long Island, she and I loved to swim in the ocean. As we walked toward the water and waded in, I eyed the breaking waves with excitement and a tinge of nervousness. Once we got through the breakers, we could swim in the gently rolling swells of the Atlantic.

One day, as I was flipping through the pages of a large boating book, a photo of Tillamook Head Lighthouse caught my eye—and my imagination. It was way across the country, off the rocky coast of Oregon, and sat more than a mile offshore on an enormous rock. Although the lighthouse was built 133 feet above the ocean, storms have been known to send breakers over its rocky perch and even toss rocks high enough to shatter the lens. Amazing! I even painted a picture of it, never dreaming I'd have the chance to see it in person.

Now this East Coast girl lives in a suburb of Seattle. One summer, my friend, Jan, invited me down to the charming town of Cannon Beach, Oregon. When I saw Tillamook Head Lighthouse off the coast, I could hardly believe it.

From my home, it's easy to get to Puget Sound and the waves of the Pacific Ocean are only a few hours away by car. Beautiful lakes are nearby. The very sight of one of them often causes me to take a deep, relaxing breath.

Several summers ago, I tried paddleboarding and realized what an easy, affordable way it was to get out on the water. Now, summer days often find me paddling around a nearby lake, happy as a clam.

I feel most at home and at peace when I am in, on, or near the water, regardless of what state or country the water may be in. Once I was out of town and deeply troubled. I took a walk to a nearby river. As I watched the water flowing along, the words of Jesus came clearly to mind: "Peace I leave with you; my peace I give you. I do not give to you as the world gives. Do not let your hearts be troubled and do not be afraid" (John 14:27). Remembering those words of Jesus, as the river gurgled nearby, brought much-needed calm to my soul.

LORD OF CREATION,

Thank you for water for drinking, cleansing, transportation, relaxation, and recreation.
Thank you for water so fish can swim, crops can grow, and so our bodies can be nourished.
Thank you for water so rivers can flow, waves can splash, waterfalls can roar, and our souls can be nourished. Amen.

CHAPTER 1—DIVING DEEPER

REFLECT

1. What sort of soundtrack would be appropriate for your own water stories?

2. What memories involving water did this chapter stir up? What feelings are associated with them? How do these memories affect you now?

3. Have you had any experiences involving water that have transcended everyday life and brought you peace or spoke to you of the Creator?

GIVE THANKS

Think about the water you see at home, at work, or on your commute. You may not have a jaw-dropping view, but is there a pond, fountain, or fish tank? Even if your only view is a glass of cool, clear water, pause for a moment to appreciate it.

Consider *all* the ways water touches your daily life. Does your morning routine include a shower and a hot cup of coffee or tea? Do you enjoy a relaxing evening bath? Do you participate in water aerobics or take your child to swim lessons? Thank God for the water that gives life and health to you.

READ

Mightier than the thunder of the great waters, mightier than the breakers of the sea—the LORD on high is mighty (Ps 93:4).

Exod 14—The Israelites cross the sea to freedom

Matt 8:23-28—Jesus calms the storm and confuses the disciples

Matt 14:22-33—Peter attempts to walk on water

ACT

During one day, or even just half a day, write down every way you interact with water. When you consider your list, what surprises you?

If you like, you can create a mini water feature for your table. Here's a simple idea: take a clear bowl, fill it with water, and float some candles or flowers in it.

There are many organizations working to provide clean drinking water for people, or to benefit the ocean and its creatures. If you are not already familiar with one, choose one to learn about. If their work appeals to you, consider supporting their efforts—alone or as a group.

Chapter 2

Beach Creatures

*To be yourself in a world that is constantly trying to make you
something else is the greatest accomplishment.*

RALPH WALDO EMERSON

PART OF THE FUN of going down to the water is seeing the variety
of life there. This is particularly true at the ocean. You may enjoy
picking up shells. Perhaps you'll catch a glimpse of a crab scurrying sideways across the sand. Or you can wander over to a tide
pool to observe starfish and sea anemones in a variety of colors.

While the deepest parts of the sea are home to some of the
most astonishing creatures on the planet, the more familiar ones
are striking, too. Picture a lobster. Imagine the back, looking like
a suit of armor, the five sets of legs, and the fan tale. The front legs
of an American lobster end in those iconic oversized claws. What
color are you picturing? Lobsters can be green, yellow, or even
bright blue, but they all turn red when cooked. They can swim
forward or backward, and will use their tails to scoot quickly in
reverse when frightened. What remarkable creatures!

As a child, I remember seeing horseshoe crabs on the beaches of Long Island. (To be scientifically accurate, they're actually
not classified as crabs, but the name isn't all wrong—their large

shells are, indeed, horseshoe-shaped.) I thought they were creepy-looking, especially with the long, pointy spike they have instead of a tail. Recently, I learned it's called a telson, and as dangerous as it looks, the purpose is simply to help the critter turn over if a wave flips it onto its back. I guess you could say it carries its own spatula! I wonder if it's hard to sneak up on a horseshoe crab, because they have nine eyes, plus light receptors. They look pre-historic. Indeed, the species has been around for so long they are considered living fossils. And there is something extraordinary about horseshoe crabs, which you would never guess by looking at their muddy-brown shells. Their blood is sky-blue, and has such strong anti-bacterial properties that a derivative is used to check for contamination in pharmaceuticals and medical devices. These scary-looking creatures actually contribute to saving lives.

From tiny fish to huge whales, birds, jellyfish, and sea lions, there certainly are a wide variety of interesting creatures that can be seen from the beach. And you, my friend, whether you happen to be reading this on the beach or anywhere else, are also a unique creation, handmade by God, in God's own image. You have gifts, talents, and vulnerabilities others may not have. You are one of a kind, valuable, and loved more than you know.

Ponder for a moment the complexity of the human body. It is truly amazing. All those moving parts! Some of our joints move not only back and forth, but also in a circular motion. Our brains control our bodily functions, process the five senses, and generate all kinds of interesting ideas. We can run on a variety of fuels—fruits and vegetables, grains, meats, even saltwater taffy! (Just don't make taffy the mainstay of your diet.)

Each person has distinguishing physical characteristics. Even identical twins are not exactly the same. Think of a characteristic that is uniquely yours, and worth celebrating. Do you have your grandfather's kind eyes? Do you have a warm smile or an infectious laugh?

Most of us tend to focus on whichever of our own physical characteristics we think are least attractive. I have read that in Scandinavian cultures, people view their bodies a little differently than we do in the United States. For example, to them, the primary purpose of legs is not to model shorts—legs are for walking! If yours can carry you up a hill, that is something to rejoice in.

Not only does each person have unique physical traits, each of us has individual character traits. Characteristics we think of as positive often seem to come along with those we view more negatively. You're highly organized? You will also be too rigid at times. You care deeply about others? You may be more susceptible to depression. We need to give ourselves grace.

The difference between a good characteristic and a negative one can be simply a matter of degree—or even of perception. In fact, they can be opposite sides of the same coin. Consider these adjectives: determined/stubborn, spontaneous/impetuous, confident/egotistical. The words in each pair are similar, and yet one has a positive connotation and the other has a negative one.

Traits that are a benefit in one environment can be a liability in another. For example, my husband makes decisions quickly and tends to stick with them. He is very routine-oriented. I'm more of a free spirit. At home, his methodical ways make him efficient and dependable. He can be sitting down with his morning coffee already, while I'm still standing in the middle of the kitchen, bleary-eyed, trying to decide if I feel like having coffee or tea. He feeds the dog her breakfast like clockwork, so regularly that we joke he will continue putting food in the dog's bowl each morning even after we no longer have the dog. On the other hand, when I give the dog her dinner, I'm easily distracted and she might have to wait a few minutes. (Yeah, I think the dog might like my husband better.)

When my husband and I travel, things are not as predictable as at home. Flight schedules change, new information is learned, and carefully made plans need to be adjusted. In these situations, my husband's preference for routine and dislike of revisiting decisions becomes a liability. You know those old GPS systems we used to use for directions? Remember how if you deviated from the directions it gave, it would start to sound cranky as it kept repeating, "recalculating"? That's my husband. Readjusting is stressful for him, whereas it's usually easy for me to be flexible. I can adapt to changes and come up with lots of options. But then I have trouble deciding between them! As I said, no one has *all* the characteristics best suited to every situation! (And not to worry, my husband has seen and "approved this message.")

In the introduction, I mentioned my dear friend Kathy, one of my beach buddies. Kathy and I have been friends since elementary school, when she moved into my neighborhood on Long Island. Later, Kathy moved to the Midwest, yet her speech retains the charming accent of her native Rhode Island. Kathy has a great ability to laugh at herself and find humor in the everyday. She has a big heart and a special love for children and the elderly. Although Kathy has lived through some daunting experiences, she faces life with courage, faith and gratitude. There is much to celebrate about her.

A few years ago, Kathy surprised me by saying she felt that, in order to be a Christian woman, she had to give up being herself. She thought she needed to fit a certain mold. I was saddened that Kathy felt that way, but grateful she shared her thoughts so I could offer encouragement. I reminded her that God loves her for the unique, wonderful woman she is. Jeremiah 1:5 says, "Before I formed you in the womb I knew you, before you were born I set you apart." And Psalms tell us the LORD takes delight in his people (18:19; 147:11; 149:4). I shared with Kathy my deep conviction that her Creator wants her to be the best "Kathy" she can be, but no one else. What a loss it would be if she exchanged her unique and delightful self for a cookie-cutter version of what she thought she was supposed to be!

Each person has a specific combination of gifts and a particular role to fill in God's kingdom. We'd all be more content if we focused less on comparing ourselves to others and more on being the best possible version of ourselves. Next time you're tempted to think or say, "I'm so _____ [insert negative adjective]," try to think of when that aspect of your personality was helpful or if there's another quality you have that balances it. Celebrate your strengths and be gentle with yourself when you recognize weaknesses. You are a wonderful creation of God!

As we learn to recognize and be thankful for our own strengths, and accept God's loving grace for our shortcomings, we may also find it easier to celebrate the gifts of others and extend grace to them.

Lord of creation,
Thank you for the uniqueness of all your creatures and for
what they show us about you. Let the magnificence of a whale,
the grace of a porpoise, the playfulness of a sea otter, and the
quirkiness of a lobster all lead us to praise you! Help me to be
the best "me" that I can be, and to fill the distinctive role you
planned for me. Amen.

CHAPTER 2—DIVING DEEPER

REFLECT

1. What makes me unique in my neighborhood, group, or community? Do I have a trait or experience no one else can claim?
2. What are my strengths? Am I using these for the benefit of others?
3. What are my weaknesses? Are they the flip side of my strengths?
4. What are my quirks? Do I need to embrace these or work on them?

GIVE THANKS

We can each pray with King David: "I praise you because I am fearfully and wonderfully made; your works are wonderful, I know that full well" (Ps 139:14).

Thank God for three specific traits or abilities you have.

READ

The LORD will fulfill his purpose for me;
Your steadfast love, O LORD, endures forever.
Do not forsake the work of your hands. (Ps 138:8 ESV)

Ps 139—LORD, you know me

1 Cor 12:1-11—gifts of the Spirit

Eph 2:10—God's handiwork

ACT

Ask God to help you see how your gifts are being used, or could be used, for the kingdom.

Express admiration for someone's abilities that are different from yours.

Tell a loved one how a little quirk of theirs makes your heart smile.

Chapter 3

BRING A FRIEND

There are good ships and wood ships,
ships that sail the sea;
but the best ships are friendships,
may they always be!

IRISH PROVERB

ONE OF MY FAVORITE friends to bring to the beach is our dog,
Abbey. She's a loveable and goofy shelter dog. She loves to run in
big circles, doing what my daughter calls "her NASCAR impressions." She's so fast we've often joked her breed mix must include
some Cheetah! Once my family was walking along an ocean beach,
with Abbey scampering nearby in the surf, when we saw a young
man out for a run. Suddenly, a golden blur on four legs zoomed
past him. Abbey sprinted by so quickly the poor runner looked
like he was standing still. To this day, we laugh as we remember
the look of utter bewilderment on his face. He got a humbling reminder that humans may be smart, but are hardly the fastest of
God's creatures!

As much as I enjoy having my dog at the beach, I usually
invite a human friend or two to share the experience as well. If you
are reading this book on your own, you might consider inviting

someone to join you as you continue to journey through these pages.

In considering friendship, I can think of no better starting place than the book of Genesis, which means "beginnings." The book opens with the story of creation. After each act of creation, we find the reassuring refrain, "And God saw that it was good." In fact, the first chapter ends with the words, "God saw all that he had made, and it was *very* good." But in chapter 2, God said something was "not good." Creation was a pristine reflection of the Creator. What could possibly be lacking? "The LORD God said, "It is not good for the man to be alone . . . " (Gen 2:18). Biology and neuroscience tell us the same thing. We were made for relationship.

Technology, which was designed to keep us connected, can isolate us. When email, texting, and social media replace being present with another person, we have lost something vital. An emoji can never replace a warm smile or hug, and hastily written words, devoid of tone and visual cues, are more prone to misunderstanding than face-to-face communication.

Since we are social beings, we have in common the yearning to feel loved, yet we have different ways of expressing love. When we don't recognize how others are showing their affection, or assume everyone knows what makes us feel cared about, hurt feelings can easily result. However, if we pay attention to what makes others smile, and are willing to be open about our own preferences, we can have fun with the many ways of showing loving care for one another.

There was much wisdom in the children's TV show *Mr. Rogers' Neighborhood*. I especially loved a song Fred Rogers used to sing, "There Are Many Ways to Say 'I Love You.'" One of the lines says "the cooking way." When my husband is preparing a nice dinner, or my daughter is putting the finishing touches on a picture-perfect holiday dessert, I find Mr. Rogers's song going through my head.

There are, indeed, countless ways to show our love. For example, I just finished hanging Christmas lights outside. December is such a busy time for me as a music teacher and church musician that I was tempted to skip it. But our daughter is coming home and she wants to see our home lighted up. As I untangled the strings and hung the lights, it felt less like doing a chore and more like giving a gift. It was a way to show our daughter how loved she is by making her homecoming bright.

Relationships are all about balancing what we have in common and what makes each person unique. My friend and ministry partner, Jan, and I enjoy being together and have a lot in common. However, since we have been working together in ministry, we have also become more aware of our differences. Having distinct individual strengths means that as a team we have competence in more areas than either of us has alone. But it is challenging when we are working toward the same goal and each of us has a natural tendency to approach it from a different direction. Jan and I strive to honor our differences and work together by listening and adjusting. Perhaps it helps that those are skills we have both honed as musicians.

As I write this, my students have just put on a holiday music recital. A highlight was a performance by two brothers, one playing violin and the other accompanying on piano. They sounded great. I love it when different instruments, each with a unique tone, play well together. But let me tell you, we had some rough rehearsals. At first, one brother or the other would not count correctly, and the whole piece would derail. As they practiced, however, not only did each improve his own playing, he also began to hear how his part fit into the piece as a whole. They listened to each other and began to adjust to one another. In the last rehearsal, there was a glitch, but they were able to pull it back together and keep going. I was so pleased. Knowing they can make a mistake, adjust, and continue gives me more confidence about the performance than if the practice goes perfectly, and I told them so. The reality is, whether in a musical performance or in life, things do go wrong. Mistakes happen. There are misunderstandings and disagreements. When we are willing to work through these rough spots with patience and a loving, listening ear, we can learn about each other and the relationship can grow.

Relationships enrich our lives and can even save our lives. Perhaps no one has stated this better than the author of Ecclesiastes. *"Two people are better off than one, for they can help each other succeed. If one person falls, the other can reach out and help. But someone who falls alone is in real trouble. Three are even better, for a triple-braided cord is not easily broken"* (Eccl 4:9–10, 12b NLT).

Lord God,
you created us for fellowship with you
and each other. You yourself said,
"It is not good for the man to be alone."
Thank you for the people around us
who give us a glimpse of your love.
*Help us to **have** supportive friends*
*and to **be** supportive friends. Amen.*

CHAPTER 3—DIVING DEEPER

REFLECT

1. How have friends/family contributed to your self-understanding and self-acceptance?

2. What are reasons people avoid being with others? When and why is it sometimes important to be alone?

3. Think of someone who has helped rekindle your faith in God, your faith in humanity, and/or your faith in yourself at a dark time in your life. Consider sharing the story with your group.

GIVE THANKS

~ for those who help you through life's rough patches.

~ for those who celebrate with you.

~ for those who greet you with a hug and a smile (or a tail wag), and make you laugh.

READ

"A friend loves at all times, and a brother is born for adversity" (Prov 17:17).

See what additional wise words about friendship you can find in the book of Proverbs, especially in chapters 17, 18, 22, and 27.

ACT

Express your appreciation to anyone who came to mind in the Give Thanks section. Write a note, send or bring flowers, bake something, treat them to lunch, or whatever seems appropriate.

Look for opportunities to brighten someone else's day today. It can be as simple as sharing a warm smile.

Chapter 4

COMMUNITY

How good and pleasant it is when God's people
live together in unity!

PSALM 133:1

COMMUNITY IS OFTEN HARD to find in today's world. We cannot pick up a newspaper without seeing words like "bitterly divided" or "polarized." It seems we have lost sight of our commonality and all we see are differences. In this setting, we wonder if it is even possible to develop community.

When disagreements arise, it's important to remember that none of us have all the answers, and we have a lot to learn from each other. Usually, differences are small compared to what we share. And if we feel we must stand firm on a certain issue, we can do so prayerfully and humbly, remembering we are called to treat each other with love.

Whether within a community of faith, our town, our nation, or our world, people have a tendency to get stuck taking sides on issues, thinking one position must be right and the other wrong.

Sometimes, what we view as a crucial issue may turn out later to be far less important than we thought. There's an interesting example of this in the well-known story of Jesus talking with the Samaritan woman at the well (John 4). Once the woman recognized Jesus as a prophet, she sought his opinion on a divisive issue of that time. The Samaritans were worshipping on nearby Mt. Gerizim, but others insisted worship must be at the temple in Jerusalem. Jesus did not respond by taking sides. With his eternal perspective, he knew this would soon be a nonissue. He told her, "A time is coming when you will worship the Father neither on this mountain nor in Jerusalem" (v. 21). The sad fact was that within forty years, the temple in Jerusalem would be utterly destroyed and the people scattered.

One way to build community is to take a step back from the issue we disagree on and spend some time getting to know each other. Certainly, there is commonality to be found in the human condition. When each person feels heard and respected, this leads to increased trust, lowering our personal defenses, and putting us on the path toward healing our divisions.

When we are ready to turn to the topic of concern, it will be more pleasant and productive if we can put our own agendas aside and develop the mindset that we are *all* problem-solvers working together. We can take a tip from Nelson Mandela, who found even enemies could be turned into partners by working together.

If we can be honest enough to share our needs and our wants, our hopes and dreams on a topic, and listen to one another, we may be surprised to find just how much we agree on. It's possible we actually agree on the ultimate *goal*—we just got entrenched in different ideas of how to achieve it. Even on hot-button issues, if we can look beneath our divisions and find common ground, we can work together to make the world a better place and build community in the process.

Let's consider relationships within the community of faith. I once heard a pastor comment that the problem with Christianity in the US today is the attitude that "it's all about me and Jesus." That mindset may arise from an American cultural emphasis on individualism, but I don't think it comes from the Bible. In the Hebrew Scriptures (Old Testament), individuals did have personal relationships with God; however, the main emphasis was on the people of Israel as a community. Jesus, too, stressed the importance of community when he said, "Where two or three gather in my name, there am I with them" (Matt 18:20), and instructed his followers to "Love one another" (John 13:34).

Relationships were certainly important to the apostle Paul. He has given us two different analogies to help his readers understand the church as a community and how each individual fits within it. For one illustration, he used something that would have been a daily sight for his readers—a stone building. Each stone was hand-cut and unique. And each stone was part of something greater. So, too, God's people join together like a building, with Jesus as the cornerstone (Eph 2:19–22). In writing to the church he founded in Corinth, Paul used the analogy of the church as a body, calling it the body of Christ. As he drives home this idea of one body with many parts, Paul's imagery becomes almost comical. "If the whole body were an eye, where would the sense of hearing be? If the whole body were an ear, where would the sense of smell be?" (1 Cor 12:17) Just as different parts of the body have different purposes, so each person has a unique and important role to play within the community.

Paul also reminds us: "There are different kinds of gifts, but the same Spirit distributes them. There are different kinds of service, but the same Lord. There are different kinds of working, but in all of them and in everyone it is the same God at work." Then Paul tells his readers what the purpose of all this is. "Now to each one the manifestation of the Spirit is given *for the common good*" (1 Cor 12:4–7) (emphasis mine). The whole community is enriched when we share our various gifts.

Father God,
Thank you for the variety of gifts you give your people.
Help us to approach differences with a listening ear and a
caring heart,
that we might work together to further your kingdom of peace.
Amen.

CHAPTER 4—DIVING DEEPER

REFLECT

1. This chapter and the previous one included different images of individuals in community: stones in a building, parts of a body, and musicians playing together. How have these pictures given you fresh perspective?

2. In Hebrews 10:25, Paul writes,

   "Let us not give up meeting together, as some are in the habit of doing, but let us encourage one another—and all the more as you see the Day approaching."

   Are there times you are tempted to give up meeting with others? How can you encourage others?

GIVE THANKS

If you have a community—or more than one—that has stuck with you through the hard times, rejoiced with you in the good times, or just made the everyday a bit more joyful, you are blessed indeed. This could be the neighbors at the bus stop, an exercise group, or a Bible study group. Let them know you appreciate them!

READ

"Be completely humble and gentle; be patient, bearing with one another in love" (Eph 4:2).

Eph 4:1–7—more of Paul's thoughts on unity

1 Cor 12, 13—spiritual gifts, love

Rom 12:18; 14:19—Paul's thoughts on living in peace

ACT

Ask God to show you a person needing your encouragement. Then welcome the new employee, thank the weary wait staff, applaud a child's efforts, etc.

Think of someone you often disagree with. Make it a point to look for some common ground with that person this week.

Chapter 5

SUNGLASSES

Look to the LORD and his strength; seek his face always.

PSALM 105:4

DO YOU KNOW WHAT US city sells the most sunglasses? Perhaps Miami, Phoenix, or Los Angeles? Nope—it's Seattle! The explanation I heard is that after a long winter of clouds and rain, no one can find their sunglasses when the sun finally comes out again, so they buy new ones.

Sunglasses are going to represent our vision as we consider perception, viewpoint, and focal point.

PERCEPTION—THE LENS WE LOOK THROUGH

Funny things can happen when we forget we're looking through sunglasses. Yesterday, as I drove along the lake, my eyes fell on a large home that is nearing completion. "*What? When did they paint that pink?*" I wondered. Then I remembered the tinted sunglasses I was wearing. Lifting my shades revealed the house was still tan.

Just as each pair of sunglasses has a slightly different tint, so each of us has a unique way of viewing the world. Our personality, faith, and life experiences all influence the lens we naturally look through. Sometimes our health, mood, and energy level affect our vision, too. I remember a pastor's wife admitting, with self-deprecating humor, how her view of her children could go from *what little darlings* to *what little slobs*, depending solely on her shifting hormone levels! I'm sure she was a better mom because she recognized the change was not in her children as much as in her perception.

Often our perception is colored by past experiences. I had a clear demonstration of this several years ago. I was in a teacher's lounge, waiting for my lunch to finish heating, when I smelled something. Looking up, I saw a wisp of smoke coming from the microwave and quickly turned it off. I must have overestimated how long it would take to heat my food. Oops. These things happen, right? But when another teacher noticed the smell, she yelled, "Smoke!" She was so upset she was shaking. I assured her it was just my lunch and apologized for the smell. She glared at me. I didn't say anything more, but wondered why she was making such a big deal out of it. Then another teacher told me the woman had recently had a house fire. *Oh.* While I was picturing an overcooked lunch, in her mind's eye she was seeing her home in flames and her family in danger. Obviously, the trauma she had experienced affected how she perceived, and responded to, my burned lunch.

Seeing our present through the lens of the past can be particularly troublesome when our perceptions have their roots in childhood. We may carry unresolved pain with us without even clearly remembering the original events. I must admit, I have come to recognize that sometimes the relationship I had with my father as a child affects the way I react to my husband's behavior.

I have had other people's childhood issues projected onto me, as well. Once I was talking with a friend and offering support when something I said offended her. I tried to clear things up by explaining what I meant. She was still angry, and I was perplexed until she said, "My mother used to say that." I suddenly understood that in those particular words she could only hear her mother's critical tone. Sometimes a person's reaction to us really isn't about us. That knowledge helps us to not take everything personally and to be more compassionate.

As humans, we can never see with perfect clarity. Fortunately, God is not like that. Isaiah 55:9 states, "'For my thoughts are not your thoughts, neither are your ways my ways,' declares the LORD. 'As the heavens are higher than the earth, so are my ways higher than your ways and my thoughts than your thoughts.'"

VIEWPOINT—THE ANGLE WE LOOK FROM

The personal lens we look through may affect our first impressions, but we can choose to try looking at things from a different viewpoint.

This morning I had plenty of time to think about viewpoint during a two-hour procedure at the periodontist's office. I don't know about you, but I'm not a fan of having hypodermic needles and sharp instruments poked into and around my gums. Besides, after the first hour, my stomach began to growl and my neck ached. I could easily think of 500 places I would have rather been than in that chair. There wasn't even a TV for distraction. However, sitting there thinking, "*I hate this. I hate this,*" was not going to help anyone, so I chose to look at things from a different angle.

I reminded myself that while the procedure was certainly not for my *enjoyment*, it was for my good. I was thankful for easy access to quality healthcare. I appreciated the kind hygienist who was putting her training to use for my benefit, and consciously thought of her hands as bringing care and healing rather than inflicting mild torture. As I shifted my viewpoint, something changed in me. No, it still wasn't fun, but I began to relax, and my discomfort seemed to ease.

Sometimes we get so focused on a problem that it begins to eclipse everything else and we lose perspective. When I realize I'm mountain climbing over a molehill, I ask myself, "*Will this matter a year from now?*" More often than not, I have to admit I won't even remember the situation in a year! Taking a broader viewpoint and looking past our present struggles can help us get through them.

We can also ask our loving heavenly Father to help us see things as he does. In the hymn, "Loving Spirit," Shirley Erena Murray painted a beautiful picture with these words: *Like a father you protect me, teach me the discerning eye, hoist me up upon your shoulder, let me see the world from high.** When we let our heavenly Father carry us, we feel his love, we glimpse eternity, and our perspective shifts.

FOCAL POINT—WHAT WE FOCUS ON

You know how some sunglasses have reflective lenses and you can't see the wearer's eyes? Recently, someone told me she wears sunglasses like that. Then when she puts on her regular glasses, she forgets which ones she's wearing and thinks people can't see who or what she's staring at. Whether others can see where we're looking or not, what we focus on is crucial.

I understand that drivers need to be careful, as there is a tendency to steer toward whatever we are looking at. In life, too, we may find ourselves moving toward what we focus on.

There's a story I read that I'd like to share with you.

> *An old Cherokee is sitting by the fire with his grandson. He gazes at the boy, and then begins to speak. "A fight is going on inside me," he tells the boy. "It is a terrible fight between two wolves. One is evil—he is anger, envy, guilt, greed, arrogance, lies, and ego." The boy's eyes grow wider, and the grandfather continues, "The other is good—he is joy, peace, love, hope, serenity, humility, kindness, truth, compassion, and faith. The same fight is going on inside each person."*
>
> *The boy stares silently at the fire for a long while before asking, "Which wolf will win?" The old Cherokee simply replies, "The one you feed."*

EYES OF FAITH

When we focus on God, his Spirit opens the eyes of our hearts. His word sheds light, altering our perception and shifting our viewpoint. It is then we begin to see with the eyes of faith. We begin to trust, even when we cannot see. Or, in Paul's words, "We live by faith, not by sight" (2 Cor 5:7).

This can be hard for us world-weary adults. Jesus often pointed to the faith of children as an example. Yesterday, my "four-legged child" provided an illustration of the trust that is at the heart of such faith. I was preparing to leave and Abbey-dog knew she would be allowed to come along. She eagerly ran to the car and waited for me to open the back so she could jump in. As I looked at her, all bright eyes and wagging tail, it occurred to me she had absolutely no idea where we were going. It could be a grand adventure, or a trip to the vet for shots. All Abbey knew was that she wanted to be with me. She trusted that wherever we went, I would take care of her needs. She knows I love her. Her trust is so complete that I doubt it ever crossed her doggy mind to wonder or worry. Why is it so hard for me to trust my heavenly Father like that?!

Let us pray, using the words of an old Irish hymn:

"Be thou my vision, O Lord of my heart;
naught be all else to me, save that thou art:
thou my best thought both by day and by night,
*waking or sleeping, thy presence my light."** *

** "Be Thou My Vision." Text: Irish, 8th cent.; tr. Mary E. Byrne, 1880–1931.

CHAPTER 5—DIVING DEEPER

REFLECT

1. In this chapter we looked at *perception, viewpoint,* and *focal point*. Which one of these seems most relevant to your life now? Why?

2. Is there something in nature that changes your viewpoint—perhaps the vastness of the ocean or gazing at the night sky? Something else? Picture it in your mind's eye and describe how it speaks to you.

3. Hebrews 11:1—12:3 is sometimes called the "Faith Hall of Fame." Which person most interests you and how do you see the eyes of faith in his/her life?

GIVE THANKS

- for the gift of physical sight.
- for God's word and the Spirit, which enlighten our hearts.
- for friends who help us reframe our thoughts.

READ

"Finally, brothers and sisters, whatever is true, whatever is noble, whatever is right, whatever is pure, whatever is lovely, whatever is admirable—if anything is excellent or praiseworthy—think about such things" (Phil 4:8).

1 Cor 13:12–13—perception

John 16:33—viewpoint

Heb 12:1–2; 1 John 3:2; Ps 16:8; 25:15—focal point

2 Kgs 6:15–17—eyes of faith

ACT

Are there adjustments you could make to the way you view the world that would help you live life more joyfully? How could you put this into practice? Seek God's guidance and the wisdom of others to create a simple, achievable plan.

Chapter 6

FLIP-FLOPS

Life is really simple,
but we insist on making it complicated.

CONFUCIUS

I LIKE WEARING FLIP-FLOPS to the beach. Actually, I like the very idea of flip-flops. They are fun, not-to-be-taken-too-seriously foot-wear, barely even qualifying as shoes. And yet, they are perfectly adequate to perform the essential function of protecting your feet from hot sand, glass, or whatever else you might not want to step on. And if you do want to go barefoot, they're easy to take off and carry.

Most of all, what I like about flip-flops is they are the essence of simplicity. Life at the beach calls for what is simple, natural, unpretentious, and uncomplicated. Can you imagine watching someone trying to walk on a beach in high heels? And what's the point of carefully styling hair that may soon be wind-blown and salt-sprayed? (Ladies, repeat after me: "Mermaid hair. Don't care.")

I've heard it said that Americans always want more, and don't know the meaning of enough. Wanting more often keeps us from enjoying what we have, and getting more tends to complicate our lives. Perhaps the prevalence of flip-flops in summer indicates there's hope at least some of us do know what enough is! I guess we could take a lesson from the Swedes. I hear they hold up a concept called *lagom*, which means "just right." Flip-flops are *lagom*.

Let's think about our opening quote. To be fair, life is more complicated today than it was in Confucius's day. However, if we value simplicity, we can choose to cultivate it. Before making a commitment, I try to remember to count the cost in terms of how it may complicate my life. That doesn't necessarily mean saying no, but pausing to consider the possible implications of yes. We will revisit this idea in the next chapter as we think about what we each carry through life in our beach bag.

One way we needlessly complicate our lives is through worry. We ruminate over issues that are not our responsibility and are not in our control. We waste energy getting stressed over things that will probably never even happen. No wonder Jesus said, "So don't worry about tomorrow, for tomorrow will bring its own worries. Today's trouble is enough for today" (Matt 6:34).

Jesus exemplified the simplest of lifestyles: as a newborn, a feeding trough served as his cradle. He spent three years as an itinerant rabbi. He warned that excessive focus on worldly possessions would get in the way of seeking God's kingdom (Matt 19:16–26).

Jesus was unimpressed with long-winded, public prayers that were more about sounding pious than about relationship with God. When his disciples asked Jesus to teach them to pray, he gave us the example of the Lord's Prayer—just five verses long (Matt 6:9–13).

I think some of the greatest and most important truths are simple. But this is not to say they are *easy*. Consider this familiar statement, "all men are created equal." It is only five words. And yet, these are some of the most powerful words ever penned. It has taken our country nearly 250 years, a civil war, and much strife, to even begin to put those words into practice. It can take our heads and our hearts and every fiber of our being to live out the most simple, basic truths. The same can be said for the life of faith.

Simple is not to be confused with simplistic. A "check your brain at the door" kind of faith can be dangerous. God wants us to use the intellect he gave us to be wise, diligent, and discerning. But let's not make things more complicated than they need to be.

In Jesus's day, the religious leaders had worked out precisely how they thought every little detail of God's teachings were to be put into practice. But in their focus on the minutiae, they often missed the whole point. Jesus wanted to turn the hearts of the people back to the *spirit* of the law. He summed up most of the Hebrew Bible ("the law and the prophets") with the words, "Love the Lord your God . . . . and love your neighbor as yourself" (Luke 10:27).

Children can be an example of simplicity. Without knowing all the details, sometimes they see right to the heart of a matter. Perhaps this is what Jesus meant when he said, "Let the little children come to me, and do not hinder them, for the kingdom of heaven belongs to such as these" (Matt 19:14).

Ironically, the more I learn, the more I come back to the beautiful simplicity of the Bible message: God loves *every one* of us quirky, wonderful, and rebellious people. He desires relationship with us. And Jesus came to facilitate that relationship. When he called his disciples, he did not give them a job description or detailed employment contract. He simply said, "Come, follow me." And he extends the same invitation to us.

Lord, thank you for your love and faithfulness.
Help us keep our lives uncomplicated enough that we can focus
on what is most important,
and follow you with the simple trust of a child. Amen.

CHAPTER 6—DIVING DEEPER

REFLECT

1. What would you like to simplify in your life?
2. What advantages are there to simplifying your life?
3. What makes simplicity difficult to achieve?
4. Is there someone in your life who exemplifies simplicity? What can you learn from him/her? (Don't forget any children in your life. Even pets can instruct us here.)

GIVE THANKS

- for the simple fact of God's love.
- for the simple pleasures of your day.

READ

"Better a little with the fear of the LORD than great wealth with turmoil" (Prov 15:16).

Matt 11:25—revealed to children

Luke 10:38-42—only one thing is needed

ACT

Identify one step you will take toward enjoying more simplicity in your life.

If question 4 in the Reflect section brought someone to mind, find a way to apply something you have learned from that person.

Part II

The Beach Bag

Chapter 7

WHAT ARE YOU CARRYING?

He who would travel happily must travel light.

ANTOINE DE SAINT-EXUPERY, *WIND, SAND, AND STARS*

WHAT WE TAKE TO the beach is important. We don't want to get sunburned, or be hungry or thirsty because we didn't pack what we need. On the other hand, we don't want to carry too much. We may prefer to keep things simple.

I remember going to the beach one day when my son was a toddler. We were meeting a friend at a large state park. As soon as I arrived, I realized we should have been more specific about exactly where to meet. Unable to communicate by cell phone, I trudged up and down the beach area in the hot sun, pushing my son in a stroller that was never intended to go in the sand, with a tote full of toys hung over the handle, a beach bag over one shoulder, and a diaper bag over the other. I did eventually locate my friend, but sad to say, I barely remember our visit. The difficulty of being overburdened is what stuck in my memory.

As with going to the beach, so it is with walking through life. We each "carry" many responsibilities, commitments, and activities—some we choose, some seem to choose us. For each of us, the contents of our beach bag will be unique. Finding balance in our lives and our schedules is one of the biggest challenges we face. It is vital for us to discern what is essential in our lives, what brings meaning and joy, and what—however nice—is simply not worth the weight in time and energy.

I just finished reading Lysa Terkeurst's book, *The Best Yes: Making Wise Decisions in the Midst of Endless Demands*. She wrote that sometimes she has to say no to requests, because to say yes would also be saying yes to craziness in her life. If Lysa needed an example of what crazy looks like, she could have used one of my mornings as Exhibit A.

It was early September, and I was gearing up for another year of teaching music lessons and rehearsing with the church choir. I had also agreed to take my mother to the doctor that day. Before leaving, I needed to get a phone number from an email. Now I *know* that if I'm not careful, logging into my email account can be like being sucked into a whirlpool. But that morning I wasn't careful. When I next looked at the clock, I had ten minutes to get out of the house. And I was still in my PJs!

I threw on some clothes, then grabbed a few groceries I'd purchased for my mother, put them in a cooler, and tossed it in the back of the car. Fortunately, my dog had already been out once, because I didn't have time for her usual morning walk. I let her jump in the car too, hoping I'd get a minute to walk her later.

Arriving at my mother's building, I was only a couple of minutes late. Whew! I helped Mom into the car and we were on our way. As I turned toward her doctor's office, I began explaining why I was running late, only to realize that I was heading to the wrong doctor's office. One of my grandmother's expressions popped into my mind, "Haste makes waste." How true! I turned around, headed the other direction, and before too long, the hospital was in sight. Anxious to get my mother to her appointment, I turned into the clinic next door, where I had taken family members recently. My mother reminded me that this morning's appointment was at the main hospital. Changing direction once again, I quickly rounded a corner and heard the cooler slide across the back of the car. Finally,

I dropped my mother at the entrance to the hospital—just barely in time for her appointment—and went to find a place to park. As I got out of the car, I patted my patient dog on the head. She was shaking! The poor thing must have been traumatized by her close encounter with the very scary big-blue-cooler. (Note to self: cooler and dog do not coexist in the back of the car.) I caught up with my mother inside the hospital, and it was actually a very productive doctor's visit.

I'd like to say this is where the story ends. But after the appointment, I needed to pick up music, drop off my mother, and stop at home before attending a friend's birthday lunch. Arriving at my house, I dropped my purse in the front hall and *finally* took my dog for a quick walk. Then I put her in the house, grabbed my keys, and left again. Halfway to the restaurant I realized my purse was still in the front hall . . .

Now believe it or not, most days I really can pass for sane. So, what went wrong that day? First, I got caught up doing something I didn't need to do right then. My day had barely started and I was already behind schedule. When we're running late, it's easy to get frazzled and distracted from the task at hand (at least it is for me). Then we become inefficient, which causes further delays. With a jam-packed schedule, there's no chance to catch up, and the craziness continues.

I need to remember that when I try to be Superwoman—thinking I can do it all—I'm more likely to end up looking like Crazywoman! I am learning to allow a little extra time, because often our commitments look reasonable until something unplanned happens.

In contrast to my Crazywoman day, let me tell you about a recent day when I actually had some literal white space on my calendar. I looked forward to what I *thought* would be a relaxed-pace summer day.

As I checked email, there was a message from a good friend who wanted to stop by. She had something to tell me. I invited her for lunch and afterwards, she filled me in. It was difficult news and it was important that she was able to tell me face to face. I handed her a box of tissues, gave her a hug, and expressed my support. When my friend left, I headed out the door right behind her. During her brief visit, my mother had called. Mom had a suspected fracture and needed a ride to Urgent Care.

As the day ended, the opening line of an old song was going through my head, "What a day this has been." I was drained. I was concerned for my mother and still processing the weighty news from my friend. But I was so grateful there had been room in my day and in my life for the unexpected, and that I had been able to be there, in every sense of the word, for my friend and for my mother.

There are so many activities and commitments with which to fill our days, and our children's days. You may have heard the idiom, "good is the enemy of best." If we take on too many of these *good* activities, we cannot have *the best*—which is a balanced life, with time for the unexpected.

When my children were in elementary school, I remember receiving a guilt-inducing notice saying that without more volunteers, a certain event would be cancelled. I understand that if we really want to see something happen, sometimes we need to step up and help. So, I asked myself, *How would I feel if this didn't happen?* I realized it wouldn't matter to me or to my children, or adversely affect any of the children at the school. Now, "How would I feel if this didn't happen?" continues to be a quick litmus test for whether to consider giving of my time and energy. Even with a tradition or activity we have done for years, if no one is interested enough to carry it forward, perhaps it's time to simplify, or just let it go.

Sometimes we get weighed down by feeling responsible for that which is not our responsibility. When it comes to our children, we often need to help them and try to smooth the way for them. But we can fall into the trap of doing things for them that they need to learn to do for themselves. And when we fill the gap every time they are irresponsible, we create more work for ourselves and circumvent an opportunity for them to learn from the consequences of their actions (or inaction). When my daughter was in ballet class, sometimes she would forget to bring her ballet shoes. Even though I was short on time, I would drive home and grab her shoes for her. After a few trips, I realized I didn't need the stress of doing that. I told her that her shoes were her responsibility, and the next time she forgot them, she'd have to pay me for "taxi service." She never forgot her shoes again!

Just because there is a perceived need (whether at work, in our family, or in some other group), it does not necessarily mean it is our place to fill it. In fact, sometimes what seems crucial in the moment turns out to be inconsequential later. I like to follow this rule: If something truly is an emergency, I say a quick prayer as I jump in to help. Otherwise, I ask for time to think/pray about it. We can express interest and enthusiasm about an idea without committing ourselves to participate right away. A phone call from a committee chair does not necessarily signify a calling from God! There might even be someone else who will enjoy the responsibility, do a great job, and blossom—if we don't jump in first.

As you decide what to take on and what to take a pass on, consider what you're interested in, and where you enjoy serving. I worked with a choir director who would often say that though he sometimes arrived at choir practice tired after a long day, he would feel energized by the end of rehearsal. To him, that confirmed he was where he was supposed to be.

Before we close this chapter, it is vital that we look not only at what we carry in terms of our commitments and our schedules, but also at what we may be carrying in our hearts. An honest examination may turn up some items in our bags that are as helpful as boulders. For example, envy can weigh us down and prevent us from enjoying the gifts we have been given. Resentment can cause us to drag the pain of the past into every new day. There may be someone we need to forgive, and that person may even be the one we see in the mirror.

I would encourage you to allow the Spirit of God to shine light into the corners of your heart, and show you if there are unresolved issues to deal with, or burdens to let go of, so you can walk in freedom. As a wise (and anonymous) person said, "Sometimes you don't realize the weight of a burden you've been carrying until you feel the weight of its release."

If we learn to pack our beach bags with care—being intentional about what we carry through life—we will find we have more room and more energy for what matters most.

Our closing prayer comes straight out of Scripture:

*"Teach us to number our days, that we may gain
a heart of wisdom."* Amen.

PSALM 90:12

CHAPTER 7—DIVING DEEPER

REFLECT

Take some time to ponder, pray, and journal:

1. Do you agree that "haste makes waste"? How?
2. What is my most important calling at this time in my life? Am I prioritizing that?
3. What activities give me joy and make me feel like "I was made for this"?

GIVE THANKS

~ for the wonderful opportunities for fellowship, learning, and playing that are available to you and those around you—even though you cannot say yes to them all.

~ for the people and pets you have invited into your life, knowing the love and joy they bring outweighs the endless complications.

READ

"Therefore, since we are surrounded by such a great cloud of witnesses, let us throw off everything that hinders and the sin that so easily entangles. And let us run with perseverance the race marked out for us" (Heb. 12:1).

Prov 4:25–27—Give careful thought to your paths

ACT

Look at your calendar. Does it accurately reflect your priorities?

Ephesians 5:10 says, "Find out what pleases the Lord." The word translated "find out," means to "test, try, examine, interpret." That may take a little time. Plan some time when you can be still and discern what this means in your life.

List specific commitments and activities you have, or are considering, and pray over each one. Are there areas of your life that need more attention? Are there areas in which good enough is really fine? Is it time to add or drop an activity? If so, makes plans for how and when to make the change.

When you identify an area that you would like to make a higher priority, set aside regular time by putting it on your calendar or iPhone. Protect that time by telling yourself, or others, "I have plans."

Chapter 8

BEACH CHAIR

Somewhere there is an empty beach chair with my name on it.

THERE ARE A VARIETY of things to do at the water's edge. One of my favorites, though, is to just kick back and relax. I usually bring a beach chair. If not, I have a big beach towel in my bag. I may feel a fresh breeze and/or the warm sun, and hear a gentle splashing or the crashing of waves. I like to just breathe deeply and soak it all in. It is restorative.

I love that the word "restoration" begins with "rest." To have healthy lives, we need to find balance between work, play, and rest—as well as between service to others and slowing down to let God minister to us and speak to us.

God worked powerfully through the prophet Elijah, including a dramatic showdown in which the God of Israel was victorious over the priests of Baal. And yet, when Elijah's life was threatened shortly after that, this man of faith was overcome by fear. After escaping into the wilderness, the exhausted prophet sat down under a tree and asked God to take his life. How did God respond? God sent an angel to him with food and water. Elijah ate, drank, and rested. Then the angel came to him again and encouraged him to eat and drink some more, saying "Get up and eat, for the journey is too much for you" (1 Kgs 19:7). This story speaks volumes about our creator's recognition of our human need for food, drink, and rest.

When God gave a list of crucial guidelines for his people (popularly known as the Ten Commandments), one of those was: "Remember the Sabbath day to keep it holy." We are to work for six days, but the seventh is a Sabbath to the Lord. "For in six days the Lord made the heavens and the earth, the sea, and all that is in them, but he rested on the seventh day" (Exod 20:8–11). I wonder if God really needed to rest. Perhaps he took the day off to set an example for us.

The teaching regarding the Sabbath was not meant to be a burden, but a gift. At the time it was given, the Hebrew people had just escaped from slavery in Egypt. After seven days a week of forced labor, what could be a better gift?!

Just as our Creator knows we need rest, so Jesus knew when his disciples needed a break. This is clear in the story found in Mark 6:30–31: "The apostles gathered around Jesus and reported to him all they had done and taught. Then, because so many people were coming and going that they did not even have a chance to eat, he said to them, 'Come with me by yourselves to a quiet place and get some rest.'"

Sometimes we think that taking a break and getting some rest is selfish. But one day I had a realization as I was on an airplane, listening to the flight attendants go through their preflight spiel. Perhaps the words "Put on your own oxygen mask before assisting others" have a broader meaning. Often, the first instinct is to jump in and help others. But if we allow ourselves to become physically or emotionally run down, we can't help anybody else, least of all small children. Some of us have a whole list of people who depend on us. It's important to take care of ourselves so we can be strong *for* them and patient *with* them.

There are times when I catch myself thinking I'll relax when my to-do list is done. But the list is never done. Just like we know it's best to fuel up our cars before they run out of gas by the side of the road, isn't it preferable to give ourselves a break when we feel tired, rather than wait until we are totally exhausted? If we just keep pushing to the point of physical and emotional exhaustion, we're likely to get sick and/or cranky, and it may take a while to get our energy back.

When something isn't going well, we often think we just need to work harder. But at times the opposite is actually true. Stepping away from a problem for a little while can be a step toward resolving it. Let me give you an illustration. I have played the flute since sixth grade. As an adult, I found a teacher who showed me a better way to play. I understood exactly what she wanted me to do, and yet, every time I picked up the flute, the old muscle patterns kicked in. I finally did the only thing I could to change the way I played—I quit daily practice and put my flute away for about six weeks. When I began to play again, I was able to let the old habits go and embrace a better way of playing. Sometimes relationships, too, need a timeout or a rest, so old patterns can be broken, allowing healthier ones to be established.

At a church staff retreat, we were once asked, "Do you rest from work or work from rest?" That question was thought-provoking. We all rest to recover from the exertion of work. However, it is also true that when we are rested and refreshed, we can approach our work with energy, perspective, and creativity.

What does rest mean to you? Rest does not necessarily mean taking a nap, but it does mean taking a break from our usual work. When we play or turn to a creative pursuit, it allows us to put our usual thoughts and concerns away for a while.

At this point, I can almost hear some of you saying, "But wait. I spend my days with young children. There is no rest time." I've been there, and I hear you. But before you dismiss the idea, think about what is possible in your situation. A sweet photo I have comes to mind. You know those baby play gyms with the hanging toys? Well, in the picture, my baby girl was lying on her back, looking up at one of those, while my three-year-old son "read" to her.

Here's the back story: One day, my son stood up and declared, "All done nap." And he didn't mean just that day! Well, his napping days may have been over, but this mom was not ready to give up that little break. So, nap time became quiet time. He didn't need to sleep, he just needed to be calm and reasonably quiet. Later, when my baby girl came along, she seemed to take her cue from her older brother. On busy days, I looked forward to this respite, and I think it was good for two active children to learn to mellow out for a bit. It worked for us, but I realize you might need to do something a little different. If you are desperate for some rest, I'd encourage you to find a way to make it happen. You and your kids will be glad you did.

Rest can be as simple as stepping outside for a breath of fresh air and a moment to enjoy the beauty of creation. At an ecopsychology lecture I attended, we learned how being in nature is healthy for our minds and bodies. This was not surprising to me. After all, nature is the environment God chose to place mankind in. You know I especially love the water, but any natural setting can provide refreshment. The Japanese have a concept called forest bathing. It's a bit of an awkward translation. If you aren't familiar with the concept, it isn't about placing a bathtub out in the woods! It is about soaking in the sights, sounds, and smells of the forest.

Sometimes rest means a break from our normal routines and surroundings. Sometimes you simply need to get out of Dodge. I recently had the opportunity to get away for a few days. I knew I needed it. I didn't even need time to think so much as I needed time to NOT think. I needed time to just be, time to let my busy mind rest, while my heart was open to God. As soon as the car began rolling down the highway, it felt as if I had hit a giant reset button. I returned home with an improved attitude and renewed vitality.

The gospel writer Luke tells us a story of two sisters, Martha and Mary. Martha was right there in the presence of Jesus, and yet, she was so busy with her hostess duties that she didn't stop to be fed. She was probably physically and spiritually hungry. And she got "hangry," wondering why no one was helping her. Jesus gently pointed out that Mary, who was sitting at the Lord's feet, had made a prudent choice (Luke 10:38–42).

A crucial part of the joy and purpose of the Sabbath is having time to study God's word and just enjoy his presence—to rest in the Lord. We are more receptive to God's voice when we stop scurrying around and still the chatter in our heads. It is interesting to note that the prophet Samuel had been serving in God's temple all day, but it was at the end of the day, when he was lying down quietly, that God called to him.

Resting in the Lord can have another meaning, as well. Sometimes, when we're in over our heads, God asks us to just stop all our flailing around and let him handle things.

One of the most dramatic scenes in the entire Bible took place as the Israelites were fleeing Egypt. Remember when they were facing the Red Sea, with Pharaoh's army in hot pursuit? Talk about being stuck between a rock and a hard place! The people sarcastically asked Moses, "Was it because there were no graves in Egypt that you brought us to the desert to die?" How did Moses, God's appointed leader, respond? Did he tell the people to start swimming? Did he suggest they plead for mercy and hope to return to slavery rather than death? No. Here's what he said: "Do not be afraid. Stand firm and you will see the deliverance the Lord will bring you today. The Egyptians you see today you will never see again. The Lord will fight for you; you need only to be still" (Exod 14:8–14).

Moses had to tell the Israelites it was time to be still. Let's not wait for someone in our lives to tell us, "You look tired. Why don't you take a break?" That may not happen. It is our own responsibility to be good stewards of our health and energy by including rest as a cherished part of the rhythm of our lives.

Dear LORD,
Help us to be tuned in to your voice, not only when you are
calling us to serve, but when you are calling us to simply come
into your presence and rest. Amen.

CHAPTER 8—DIVING DEEPER

REFLECT

1. When I have a chance to rest, I love to get a mug of a favorite drink, maybe light a candle, and read a book. Yet, when I get worn out at the end of the day, I often find myself just staring at whatever's on TV, or window shopping online. It would be helpful for me to be more intentional about planning a break. How about you?

2. Ecclesiastes 4:6 states, "Better one handful with tranquility than two handfuls with toil and chasing the wind." Proverbs 23:4–5 reads, "Do not wear yourself out to get rich; do not trust your own cleverness." What do these verses mean to you?

3. What type of sea creature are we likely to resemble if we don't take time for rest? (A crab! Haha.)

GIVE THANKS

- for the most restful spot in your home or yard.
- for your favorite place to get away.
- for God's invitation to "be still and know that I am God" (Ps 46:10).

Even as we long for rest, or plan a break, let's take a moment and thank God for the many blessings that keep us busy, such as employment, family, and a place to call home!

READ

"Come to me, all you who are weary and burdened, and
I will give you rest" (Matt 11:28).

Ps 62:5—Find rest in God.

Ps 46:10—"Be still and know . . . "

ACT

Do you feel the need for daily short breaks and/or a vacation? Take
some steps toward making that a reality.

Do you know someone else who really needs a rest? Can you help
facilitate that? You could babysit for an hour so a new mom can
catch a nap, or take the children of a single parent to the park for
an hour. Perhaps you can visit with an elderly neighbor while the
care-giving spouse takes a break.

Chapter 9

LIFE RING

Prayer keeps us afloat.

JAN "FALPH" ABRAHAMSON-LISCOM

A LIFE PRESERVER RING is a great thing to have near the water. On a pleasant day you can float around, resting on it. In case of emergency, you can grab on to it for dear life. Prayer, too, is intended for everyday needs, as well as emergencies. At a Beach Walk Ministries retreat in Nebraska, one of the wonderful women there also observed that prayer, like the circular life ring, is never-ending. Indeed, the apostle Paul said, "Pray continually" (1 Thess 5:17). We can pray at any time, silently or aloud. We can journal our prayers, essentially writing a letter to God. (This practice helps me slow down, focus, and be present.) We can pray alone, with a friend, or in a group. Some people pray while they walk. Others stand, kneel, bow, or sit. Abraham, Moses, Aaron, and Jesus some-times fell on their faces before God, their very posture expressing recognition of God's sovereignty, submission before him, and de-pendence on him.

Prayer can be as delightfully uncomplicated as the title of Anne Lamott's book, *Help, Thanks, Wow: The Three Essential Prayers*. Or it can be as challenging as Jacob wrestling with God

(Gen 32:22–32). I know of someone who approached God in prayer for the first time, with the hesitant words, "Umm . . . s'up?" I suspect that God smiled, just pleased that the young man had approached him. (While respect and humility are appropriate in approaching God, I would submit that formality is optional!)

Prayer is simply communication with God. As in any relationship, communication is essential but not always easy. And for a relationship to thrive, communication must be honest. In fact, honesty is a hallmark of a relationship built on love and trust. We can see this played out in the lives of Abraham and Moses. God referred to the first as "Abraham my friend" (Isa 41:8). Of Moses, Scripture says, "The LORD would speak to Moses face to face, as one speaks to a friend" (Exod 33:11). Both of these men were quite candid with God, who has never been afraid of the doubts or questions of his people. He already knows what's in our hearts, anyway. It's also important to be honest with ourselves. For example, if we ask for guidance, we need to be willing to listen and follow it.

When we begin a conversation with God, the first question is how to address the Holy One. Beyond "S'up?," different individuals, and different traditions, emphasize awe, familiarity, or both. I love the soaring words that begin Hebrew prayers of blessing, "Blessed are You, LORD, our God, King of the Universe (*Baruch Ata Adonai Eloheynu Melech Haolam)*." A Jewish prayer for the High Holidays begins every petition with the words "Our Father, Our King" *(Avinu Malkeinu)*. Those words cause me to pause and consider: *What does it mean to acknowledge God as both parent and king?* I also love the intimacy expressed when Jesus called his father *Abba*. This must have shocked his first listeners, as *Abba* does not simply mean "Father." It is the cry of a young child's heart, "Daddy." And Paul tells us that we can approach God in the same way (Rom 8:15; Gal 4:6).

Let's look at the opening words of the Lord's Prayer, which Jesus offered as a model when his disciples asked him to teach them to pray (Matt 6:9–13): "Our Father" (signifying a relationship of love and trust) "in heaven" (a reminder that this is not a mere mortal we're talking to). For myself, I often begin prayers by addressing God as "Lord." In doing so, I acknowledge God as Lord of All—and it makes me think about whether I am truly letting him be Lord of my life.

We can stay in touch with God by means of short prayers throughout the day. When we have a more deliberate prayer time, it is good to take a few moments to center ourselves first. Just as rough water does not settle down to glassy calm the moment the wind stops blowing (except in the gospel story when Jesus commands it to), so our souls do not settle down the moment we have a little quiet. It can take a while for silence to become stillness.

Once we are settled, there are several important aspects to prayer. While not every prayer will include all of them, I like having a simple framework in mind. Some people use the acronym ACTS, which stands for Adoration, Confession, Thanksgiving, and Supplication. Whoever came up with that must have been paid by the syllable! For my children, I created my own version, which I still use: PATAL. (You can think of "Paddle," just don't spell it that way!) It stands for Praise, Apology, Thanks, Ask, and Listen. Let's explore each of these parts.

PRAISE

"Enter his gates with thanksgiving and his courts with praise" (Ps 100:4a). Praise honors God's character, as is illustrated in the next verse, "For the LORD is good and his love endures forever; his faithfulness continues through all generations." If you're not sure what to say, you can pray the words of a psalm or use one to inspire your own words.

APOLOGY

As we enter God's presence, we need to recognize both his absolute holiness and our own imperfection. When we harm animals or the earth, we have marred creation. If we have hurt another person, we have hurt someone who bears the very image of God, and owe an apology to the Creator (as well as to whomever we have wronged). But rest assured, God knows our weaknesses and still loves us. When we acknowledge where we have missed the mark of being all we are called to be, God meets us with his mercy. We can gratefully accept God's offer of forgiveness and ask for help to do better.

THANKS

We all experience many blessings each day, and it's easy to take them for granted. Recognizing them and saying thank you can help us develop a more grateful spirit. I often begin right where I am, by thanking God for the comfortable chair I'm sitting in, the roof over my head, and the trees outside the window. Then I thank him for those who share this home, and so on. Gratitude helps us focus on what we have, not what we don't have, and opens us to God's presence.

When things are going our way, it's easy to be thankful. But Paul admonishes us to "Pray continually, give thanks in *all* circumstances" (1 Thess 5:17–18). In tough situations, we have to look for points of gratitude. But notice, Paul says to give thanks *in* all circumstances, not *for* all circumstances.

Years ago, I read Corrie Ten Boom's book, *The Hiding Place*, and one story she shared particularly struck me. It is an example of giving thanks in all circumstances and of good coming from a horrible situation. She was in a Nazi prison camp *(evil!)* and the room Corrie shared became infested with fleas *(awful!)*. However, Corrie thanked God that those fleas kept the guards out. It may take some effort, but even on our worst days, we can always find something to be grateful for.

ASK

I would venture to say that this is the aspect of prayer that most people think of first. Whether in everyday events or a sudden emergency, God wants us to turn to him and talk things over. We are invited to share our joys and our tears, and ask for wisdom.

When we're uncomfortable and unhappy, it's natural to ask God to change our circumstances. However, sometimes the situation we're in can be used for our growth and/or the growth of those around us. Even when we have to live with our circumstances for a while, we can ask for the comfort of God's presence, an open mind to learn, and an open heart to trust.

Sometimes we want to pray about a situation, but hardly know where to begin. We may want to pray for someone else, but aren't sure exactly what the needs are, and are unable to ask the person. We can pray for God's will to be done, even when we don't know what God's will is. We can ask for healing and wholeness, even when we don't know whether that is best accomplished here or in heaven. And if words fail us, that's OK, too. The Quakers have a lovely expression: to pray for someone is to "hold him or her in the light." This can be done wordlessly. You can simply picture lifting that person up and letting God's light shine on him or her. Finally, it is comforting to remember that when we do not know how to pray, "The Spirit himself intercedes for us" (Rom 8:26).

When we pray, it's good to remember that God understands our situations far better than we do, and how to help us. He does not necessarily need our suggestions, since he is able "to do immeasurably more than all we ask or imagine" (Eph 3:20).

Finally, we can end this part of our prayer with another thank you: that God knows what we need before we ask, and may indeed already be at work (Matt 6:8).

LISTEN

The writer of Ecclesiastes, presumed to be the wise King Solomon, has a sobering reminder for us: "Guard your steps when you go to the house of God. *Go near to listen* rather than to offer the sacrifice of fools, who do not know that they do wrong" (Eccl 5:1) (emphasis mine). When one person does all the talking and then leaves without giving the other a chance to respond, that's not a conversation. So, too, in prayer, it's important to stop talking and listen for a bit. I have heard it said that God whispers because he wants us to draw close to hear. The more we quiet ourselves and listen for God's voice, the better we get at discerning it. However, listening for God's voice does not necessarily mean staying on our knees until we hear an audible voice, or a clear voice in our minds. We can continue actively listening after we say "Amen."

When we think God is not responding to our prayers, he may already be at work—we just don't know it yet! Waiting for the LORD is a common theme in Scripture. In English, that sounds so passive, as if we are told to just sit and twiddle our thumbs. But the Hebrew word, *kawah,* which is translated "wait," means to hope for and look for. It connotes actively watching. We see this when a child or a pet waits for someone to come home. My dog sits by the window, her posture alert and her ears perked up, wagging her tail in anticipation as she listens for the sound of a certain car motor. She is the picture of waiting with hope and expectation!

If we trust someone and know they love us, we will wait for that person. As we wait on God, it is important that we pay attention because answers often don't come in the way and the time we expect. Sometimes God uses his creation to speak to our hearts, as he did for me with the sign of the rainbow (see ch. 17). God can convey a message through the caring words of another person. And, most importantly, God has spoken and *continues to speak* through his written word, which we will reflect on in chapter 11. His voice is always consistent with the message and tone of Scripture.

Often the Bible urges us to remember what the Lord has done for us. I like to keep a journal that includes questions, struggles, prayers and insights. Looking back at my journal reminds me of God's faithfulness.

This closing prayer is designed to leave room for you to personalize it and speak with God about what's on your mind and heart today.

Let us pray . . .

Father God, we are so grateful that you want to communicate with your creation.

Thank you for the privilege of coming before you in prayer.
You are worthy of praise, for you are . . .
I am sorry for . . .
Thank you for . . .
I lift up . . .
[Take time to pause and listen.]
Help me be aware of your presence and guidance as I walk through this day and the days ahead.
Amen. (So be it!)

CHAPTER 9—DIVING DEEPER

REFLECT

1. Which aspect of prayer comes most easily to you? Which aspect is the most challenging? Why?

2. Jesus stated, "My sheep listen to my voice" (John 10:34). Do you feel you can readily hear Jesus's voice? How could you become better attuned to God's voice in your life?

3. In chapter 8, we considered rest. How do those ideas apply to your prayer life?

GIVE THANKS

∽ for God's love and care.

∽ for God's mercy.

∽ for God's nearness to all who earnestly call to him.

READ

"Call to me and I will answer you" (Jer 33:3).

"The LORD is near to all who call on him, to all who call on him in truth" (Ps 145:18).

1 Kgs 19:11–14—Elijah and the gentle whisper

2 Kgs 5:1–19a— Naaman and a healing that almost didn't happen

Hab 1:1—2:3—Habakkuk keeps watch

Ps 5:1–3—King David's prayer

ACT

Try praying in a different way than you normally do. Here are a few suggestions:

- If you find your mind tends to wander, try journaling your prayers.

- If you struggle with being thankful, keep a gratitude journal or take photos of what you are grateful for throughout the day. Later, as you look at your list or the photos, thank God for those things.

- If distractions are a problem, take steps to eliminate them. Find a quiet spot, inside or outside. Silence your phone. You might even consider a way to signal to others that you would like to be undisturbed for a little while. It could be as simple as lighting a candle (or turning on an electric one).

Chapter 10

LIP BALM

Those who guard their lips preserve their lives,
but those who speak rashly will come to ruin.

PROVERBS 13:3

THERE IS A VERY small, but important, item I always carry in my beach bag—lip balm. It's indispensable at the shore, where the sun and wind are drying. The feeling of dry lips really bugs me! I've even told my husband that if I ever get marooned on a tropical island, I'd appreciate it if he would please swim some lip balm out to me. Sometimes little things are essential!

James, the brother and apostle of Jesus, wrote about something else that is small but important. He compared the tongue to the rudder of a mighty ship whose modest size belies its influence (Jas 3:4). The rudder can determine whether the ship sails smoothly or runs aground on the rocks. Figuratively speaking, the tongue has a similar effect on relationships. In our beach bags, lip balm represents the words that come from our lips.

In the last chapter, we considered what we say to God in prayer. In this chapter, we are turning our attention to how we speak to each other. There should be some connection between the two. In the same passage we looked at above, James continues,

"With the tongue we praise our Lord and Father, and with it we curse human beings, who have been made in God's likeness. . . . My brothers, this should not be" (Jas 3:9, 10b). The incongruity of that image is jarring, and I cannot agree more—"this should not be." Spending time in our Father's loving presence should empower us to be kindhearted toward others, and to speak accordingly.

We have an amazing opportunity to be a blessing to people simply by putting our caring thoughts into words. We have the task and the privilege of encouraging one another—I know how badly I need that sometimes. That's why my blog is called *Splashes of Encouragement* (Splashesofencouragement.com).

Just a few words can help someone feel seen, heard, cared about, and supported. As you read each of these phrases, pause for a moment and consider the impact it could have.

> "Yeah, me too."
> "I'm sorry."
> "Thank you."
> "I'll go with you."
> "I'll be praying for you."
> "I'm so happy for you."
> "You're important to me."

Even just one little word is enough to make a difference. We can acknowledge someone's shock or excitement with "Wow!" or validate someone's physical or emotional pain with "Ouch!"

Like our speech, our silence can be either helpful or hurtful. Sometimes our silent presence, and perhaps a gentle touch, is better than any words we could speak. I admire people who can sit with someone who is experiencing grief or pain, and just be fully with that person, without feeling the need to talk.

On the other hand, there are times when we should speak up on behalf of others; it would be wrong to be detached and silent. Or our silence can be a missed opportunity to support or celebrate with someone. I remember when I attended a small gathering and shared the happy news that I was pregnant with our second child.

No one said anything! In the deafening silence, I was left to wonder what they might be thinking. Since our first-born was overtired and behaving poorly that night, I imagined their thoughts were *Wow. And they can't even handle one child!* To this day, I am not certain of each person's reasons for staying quiet. While I know they care about me and my family, I certainly did not feel it that night. My attitude is, this life has enough bad and sad news, so let's cheer when we hear good news!

As important as our spoken words are, what we write may be even more powerful. When we have positive, encouraging words to share, putting them in writing often makes them more effective. A handwritten note is a rare gift that can be reread any time.

In Psalm 15, King David asks, "LORD, who may dwell in your sanctuary? Who may live on your holy hill?" Then the query is answered: "He whose walk is blameless and who does what is righteous, who speaks the truth from his heart . . . who keeps his oath even when it hurts" (vv. 1–2, 4b). Don't we want people to trust that our word means something and know we will follow through?

If we want to speak and write the truth, we also need to use discretion in what we repeat. Sharing stories too readily on social media contributes to spreading rumors. Good old-fashioned gossip is often untrue, or quickly becomes untrue as it is retold. Even when it is accurate, it is not helpful, and damages relationships by breaking trust. My personal favorite guideline for healthy relationships is found in these five words of Paul, from Ephesians 4:15, "speaking the truth in love."

Have you ever sent a text or email, and then realized you sent it to the wrong person? Or you intended a comment for one person, but accidentally hit reply all? Your heart sinks as you realize what you wrote is now out there in black and white—and can be easily shared further. Last time I sent an email to the wrong person, I was so grateful it was only a *little* bit snarky. Afterwards, I determined that if I have comments that I wouldn't want passed on, it might be best not to write them, or even say them, in the first place. I can relate to David's plea, "Set a guard over my mouth, O LORD; keep watch over the door of my lips" (Ps 141:3).

Our opening quote was from David's son, King Solomon. Let's reflect on another wise saying of his: "A fool shows his annoyance at once, but a prudent man overlooks an insult" (Prov 12:16). To me, this is a reminder that it isn't necessary to react to every careless word or act. A writer friend shared this story: One day she was particularly tired and got impatient with a colleague. Next thing she knew, she had an antagonistic email from him in her inbox. Wrestling with how to respond, she resisted the urge to continue the war of words. Instead, realizing she had made plans to have lunch with this colleague, she emailed back, "Now don't think this is going to get you out of our lunch. See you in the cafeteria at noon." The working relationship was better for her discretion. Even when things do need to be addressed, Solomon's words prompt me to take the time to think and pray, so I can respond in a calm and loving manner.

In this chapter, we have used lip balm to represent our words. Besides the logical connection between our lips and our language, we also considered the small size and relative importance (at least to me!) of lip balm, and also of the tongue. There is one more parallel that can be drawn. Lip balm is healing, and our words can be, too: "Gracious words are a honeycomb, sweet to the soul and healing to the bones" (Prov 16:24).

Making use of our words for good and not for evil improves the quality of our lives and leads toward peace with those around us.

As King David wrote,

> Whoever of you loves life and desires to see many good days,
> Keep your tongue from evil and your lips from speaking lies.
> Turn from evil and do good; seek peace and pursue it.
> (Ps 34:12–14)

For our ending prayer, let us join David in saying:

"May these words of my mouth and this meditation of my heart be pleasing in your sight, LORD, my Rock and my Redeemer."

PSALM 19:14

CHAPTER 10—DIVING DEEPER

REFLECT

1. Have hurtful words been spoken to you that continue to play over in your mind? Is it possible to replace those with kinder and truer statements about yourself? Can you forgive the person who spoke unkindly to you?

2. Do you need to apologize to someone for something you have said?

3. Romans 12:15 says, "Rejoice with those who rejoice, mourn with those who mourn." What are some ways you can verbally share in another person's joy or sorrow?

GIVE THANKS

~ for a time in your life when just a few words made all the difference.

~ for friends who are honest and trustworthy.

~ for those who have shared wisdom and knowledge with you.

READ

Reckless words pierce like a sword, but the tongue of the wise brings healing (Prov 12:18).

1 Thess 5:11—encouraging others

Luke 6:45—words reflect what's in the heart

The book of Proverbs is chock full of wise sayings about our speech. See how many references you can find in these chapters: 10, 12, 15, 17, 19, 22, 25, or you may wish to go through all of Proverbs by reading a chapter a day for a month.

ACT

Do you know someone who could use a word of support, encouragement, or celebration? You could send a text or an email, but consider making the extra effort to pick up the phone and/or pick up a pen. There is power in your words.

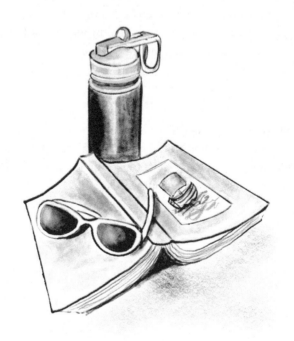

Chapter 11

GOOD BOOK

They are not just idle words for you—they are your life.

DEUTERONOMY 32:47A

I LOVE WALKING ALONG an uncrowded seaside beach. As I breathe deeply of the fresh ocean air, I can feel my spirit begin to settle down. Watching the waves roll in, I think about how they have been breaking on this shore for generation after generation and will continue long after I have gone home. My thoughts turn to God and I thank him for the beauty of his creation and his care for his creatures. I listen to the sound of the surf, the wind, and the sea gulls. While I am in this peaceful place, I want to listen for God's voice, too.

As we touched on in chapter 10, there are many ways God can speak to God's people and often it is through Scripture. When I get back to wherever I am staying at the beach, I will open the window to hear the surf and find a comfy place to sit. Then I'll pull a Bible out of my beach bag, or use the app on my phone if I'm traveling light. It never ceases to amaze me how the books of the Bible, written so long ago, can speak actively into our lives today, as part of our relationship and communication with God. I would love to share a few illustrations from my own story.

Often, if I open my Bible to wherever my bookmark is—whatever passage I have been reading or studying—I will find applications to my life at that time. But, once in a while, God will guide me to a particular section. There was one time this happened in a most unique way. My husband had been given notice that his employment was going to be ending. Although I felt that God had everything under control, my husband, who feels personally responsible for the family's finances, was understandably apprehensive. As the final day of his employment drew closer, the tension in our home was palpable. One morning as I awoke, the words "Joshua 1" were placed on my heart. While I was somewhat familiar with the book of Joshua, I couldn't remember exactly what was in the first chapter. Had I imagined those words? I didn't think so. Eagerly, I ran down the stairs and grabbed my Bible to find out what God wanted to say to me. This was like a treasure hunt!

Flipping the pages to the first chapter of Joshua, I read, "Be strong and courageous . . . " Those words appear not once or twice, but *four* times in that chapter. There are also reminders of what God asks from us and what he promises to us, including his presence. It was just what I needed to read—and marvelous reassurance for my stressed-out husband. Those words may have been written ages ago, but they were as fresh as our morning coffee! By the way, God really did have everything under control. My husband worked his old job until Good Friday. Then, on Easter, we celebrated the new life of resurrection—and his new job, which began the following day.

When I have Scriptures memorized, the Spirit can bring them to mind when I need them. Several years ago, I had been offered a new church music position. I wanted to accept, but felt it was important to pause and give God the opportunity to speak to me. It seemed right to kneel for this prayer. As I bent my knees, these words immediately came to mind, "'This is the way; walk in it'" (Isa 30:21). I took the job, and I'm so glad I did!

Clearly, I believe God has used his written word to speak to me. However, I do want to share with you, dear reader, one lesson I have learned. Especially when I have a decision to make and am anxious for guidance, I need to be careful to not hear or see just any verse that might possibly relate to my situation, think *It's a sign,* and jump to a conclusion about how I should respond. I need to continue to pray and ponder, to ensure that I am correctly understanding not only what the Scripture means, but its application to my particular situation.

How can such an ancient book be so relevant to our lives today? I believe the answer is that the Bible is different from any other book. Many people say it is inspired. But what, exactly, does "inspired" mean? For me, it came into focus when I heard that the original Greek word, *theopneustos,* can be translated as "God-breathed." I think of creation: "The LORD God formed the man from the dust of the ground and breathed into his nostrils the breath of life, and the man became a living being" (Gen 2:7). God's breath is a powerful, life-giving, and life-sustaining force! If God has breathed into Scripture, in a sense it, too, is alive. God's word is active and achieves his purposes (2 Tim 3:16; Heb 4:12; Isa 55:10–11).

The Bible is the continuous story of God's love for his people, from Genesis through Revelation. Many themes carry all the way through. As God's living Word, Jesus was with God when the law was given to Moses. He revered the Scriptures of his day, the Hebrew Scriptures. (I personally prefer that term to "the Old Testament," because "old" can sound dusty, outdated, done.) While the books of the New Testament can seem more approachable to Christians, I contend that to only read those would be like starting a movie two-thirds of the way through. You may be able to follow the plot, but will miss some of the depth of the full picture.

The sixty-six books that make up the Bible were penned by a variety of people across a time span of well over 1,000 years. They include various genres: poetic, historical, inspirational, apocalyptic, and more. I've even heard a case made that the book of Jonah is satire. The type of literature we are reading affects how we understand it. Sometimes, while we agree a certain passage is *true,* opinions differ on whether it is meant to be taken as literal truth, or as poetic or allegorical truth. Rather than fight over these differences,

I think it's more productive to focus on how the message applies to our lives.

Once I casually commented to someone that I didn't ultimately care whether Jonah was actually swallowed by a huge fish or not, because I understood the point of the story. The person I was talking with looked at me like I was an absolute *heretic*! A couple of months later, I attended a large, nondenominational Bible study. Guess who my small-group leader was?! Yup. My first thought was, *God sure has a sense of humor*, but the other woman may not have been so amused. She was probably horrified to find out this heretic was in her group. However, we studied together all year and never had an issue.

The pages of the Bible contain a treasure trove of wisdom. But it is not always easy to understand. Getting all the richness out of the Bible can require some digging, but what we find is more precious than gold (see Ps 19:10)! When I want to better grasp the full meaning of a passage, or wrestle with one that challenges me, I keep three considerations in mind: communication, culture, and context.

COMMUNICATION

We all know that not a word of the Bible was originally penned in English, but rather in the ancient languages of the Middle East. And yet, we easily forget that as words go from one language to another, the translation of a single word can impact the meaning of a whole passage. For example, sometimes we read about God *remembering*. God remembered Noah and all the animals in the ark (Gen 8:1). God heard the Hebrew slaves crying out and remembered his covenant (Exod 2:24). I first read those passages and thought, *Wait! You mean God forgot that Noah and all those animals were floating around in the ark?!* Or, *You mean his mind drifted from his people in slavery and they had to cry out to remind him of their plight?* In our language and way of thinking, remembering is an intellectual activity. If you don't remember, you must have forgotten. The passages made more sense when I realized the

Hebrew language is much more action-oriented. The Hebrew word for "remember" means to do something about it! (In the same way, the word translated "hear" means to act on what you hear.)

CULTURE

While I believe the truths of Scripture are universal, they often become clearer when we understand how a message would have sounded to the original audience. Let's say we want to grasp the full meaning of something Jesus said. It can be eye-opening to take into account what would have been on his listener's minds and what might have surprised them about what they heard.

Three factors shaped the Jewish culture of first-century Palestine. First, there was the foundation of the Hebrew Scriptures, with which the people were well acquainted. Then there were also a multitude of additional regulations and traditions. These had been developed for the purpose of clarifying how to live out scriptural injunctions, but sadly, they had begun to take on a life of their own, sometimes even overshadowing the principles they were meant to uphold. Finally, there were daily reminders that they lived in an occupied country, under the repressive rule of the Romans.

Let's explore a scene from John 7 to see how an awareness of the culture adds richness and depth to our understanding. John tells us it was during the Feast of Tabernacles. This is not superfluous information—it sets the stage. The eight-day feast, also known as Sukkot, was a well-attended, joyful remembrance of God's care for his people on their journey from Egypt to the promised land. The people would be remembering how Moses had delivered them from Egypt. How they were longing for one like him who would free them from Roman oppression! Could Jesus be the one?

On the final day of the feast, the high priest and thousands of worshippers came down from the Temple Mount and went to the pool of Siloam, where the high priest filled a pitcher with water. The shofar (ram's horn) sounded as they returned through the Water Gate, and with singing and dancing, the procession headed back up to the Temple Mount. The high priest lifted his hands and poured the water over the altar. It was a graphic reminder of how Moses had brought water out of the rock to provide for the physical thirst of the people in the wilderness. Now imagine, just as the water splashes down over the altar, hearing Jesus proclaiming himself to be the answer to their spiritual thirst. "Let anyone who is thirsty come to me and drink. Whoever believes in me, as Scripture has said, rivers of living water will flow from within them" (John 7:37–38).

CONTEXT

To understand a particular passage, it's helpful to view it within the context of the chapter and the biblical book it's in, and also see how the meaning fits with the message of the Bible as a whole. Happily, the more we read, the better able we are to let Scripture interpret Scripture. This can help us make sense of difficult sections. For me, Luke 14:26 used to be one such passage. Jesus is quoted as saying, "If anyone comes to me and does not hate his father and mother, his wife and children . . . he cannot be my disciple." That sounds harsh! I pondered other Scriptures. *Didn't God inscribe* "Honor your father and mother" *on a stone tablet for his people, and didn't Jesus specifically uphold that commandment* (Matt 15:3–9)? *How can the one who challenged us to love our enemies ask us to hate our families?* When a verse doesn't seem to line up with the concepts of Scripture as a whole, it's time to find out more. So, I looked at the cross-reference indicated in my Bible. It led me to Jesus' words in a similar passage (Matt 10:37), "Anyone who loves his father or mother more than me is not worthy of me." This could indicate a more nuanced understanding of Jesus' meaning. Returning to our first consideration, which was communication, it turns out that the Greek word, *miseo*, translated as "hate," does not necessarily connote strong negative emotion. It can simply mean to value less. So, I think it's quite reasonable to conclude Jesus wasn't telling us to *hate* our families in the way we usually think of that word, but was making the point that he is worthy of our primary allegiance. That understanding echoes the opening lines of the Ten

Commandments: "I am the LORD your God . . . You shall have no other gods before me" (Exod 20:2–3).

If you're interested in mining the depths of Scripture, please don't think it requires Greek and Hebrew classes at seminary and a shelf full of reference books! There are some resources listed in the back of this book, including a few very useful apps. It seems a bit paradoxical that twenty-first-century technology can be quite helpful in navigating this ancient text. As a t-shirt I saw recently says, "Moses was the first person with a tablet downloading data from the cloud!" Truly, the Scriptures are both ancient and ageless. After all, "The grass withers and the flowers fall, but the word of our God endures forever" (Isa 40:8).

The content of the Bible is enormous, but take heart. Like most things in life, becoming familiar with it is a process. Finally, the Bible is God's story, and God's spirit will help you understand it. Enjoy the journey and each new discovery!

Thank you, Lord God, for giving us the Bible, this story of your relationship with your people, this love letter to all who will read it. May your word take root in our hearts. Amen.

CHAPTER 11—DIVING DEEPER

REFLECT

1. Jesus said, "Man shall not live on bread alone, but on every word that comes from the mouth of God" (Matt 4:4). What similarities are there between eating for physical health, and hearing (or reading) God's word for spiritual health?

2. With many books, just reading is enough. However, with Scripture, we are encouraged to let it take root in our hearts and lives. This may include understanding, meditating on, memorizing, believing, and living out what you read. Which do you tend to focus on the most? Would attention to one of the other areas help you grow?

3. How can you make God's word an integral part of your daily life (see Deut 6:5–9)?

GIVE THANKS

⋙ to God our Father, for caring enough to give his children principles to live by.

⋙ to Jesus, for being our living Word.

⋙ to the Holy Spirit, for teaching and reminding us of all Jesus has said.

READ

As the rain and the snow come down from heaven,
and do not return to it without watering the earth and making
   it bud and flourish,
so that it yields seed for the sower and bread for the eater,
so is my word that goes out from my mouth:
It will not return to me empty, but will accomplish what I desire
and achieve the purpose for which I sent it (Isa 55:10–11).

Purposes and promises of reading, believing, memorizing, obeying:

Rom 15:4—hope

John 20:31; 6:63—life

Ps 119:11—avoid sin

Deut 12:28—go well with you and your children

ACT

Psalm 119 is the longest psalm, and it is an ode to God's word. Read carefully through it. You may wish to pray along with the psalmist.

Choose a biblical story you would like to engage with on a deeper level. Try to envision yourself in the scene. You may experience it from the standpoint of one or more of the main characters or as a bystander. Employ your senses as you imagine your surroundings. See what new insights this process gives you.

Choose a passage to memorize, such as:

Ps 117 (It's the shortest psalm—only two verses long!)

2 Tim 3:16–17—about Scripture

Chapter 12

BEACH BALL

Let me hear joy and gladness
PSALM 51:8A

THERE'S ANOTHER ITEM I want to grab to put in my beach bag. Just a moment . . .

OK, got it. It's just a simple, inflatable beach ball. It resembles a giant piece of fruit with brightly colored sections: orange, blue, yellow. It may not look like anything special, but it holds joyful memories. I think of long summer afternoons, relishing the time with my children as we played at a beach or pool. Just the sight of this ball reminds me of the feel of warm sun on my skin, and the beauty of a clear blue sky—even on the dreariest day a Seattle-area winter can dish up. One of the most wonderful scenes I could imagine would be the sight of a beach ball, tossed high into an azure sky, accompanied by children's laughter and the sounds of a gentle surf. For me, this ordinary beach ball represents joy.

What brings you joy? The smell of a rose or perhaps the taste of saltwater taffy? Sharing a meal with friends and family? The smiling face of a beloved child? If you were to draw a picture of joy, what would it look like? Maybe it wouldn't even be a specific image, but an exuberant explosion of color!

I would encourage you to pay attention to what makes your heart sing. These are the things that keep you refreshed and energized. This is important, especially if you're busy caring for others. Moreover, if you happen to be looking for ways to shine God's light and help others, knowing what you enjoy may lead you toward a type of service that you are uniquely suited for. Let's suppose you love to dig in the dirt and watch things grow. You could indulge that passion, and also make someone's day, by donating fresh produce to a local food bank or delivering a fresh-cut bouquet to a lonely neighbor.

Perhaps you'd like to incorporate more of what you love into your life, but it doesn't seem practical. Before you write off the idea, focus on what is doable in your situation. Sometimes a little creativity is required. Let's continue to imagine you love gardening—but live in an apartment. Well, could you rent a pea patch in a community garden? Or, how about offering to plant flowers at the entrance to a place of worship, a school, or your own neighborhood? Perhaps you could offer assistance to an older couple who can no longer care for their own garden. That way, you would get to spend time in your happy place—a garden—and the owners would love seeing the resulting beauty.

To be sure, joy is about far more than just finding your happy place. In fact, as I sit here writing, I can't escape the irony of the situation. Here I am, an author who sometimes battles depression, writing about joy in the midst of a global pandemic and a time of social upheaval. Today's news included a story about the physical and emotional exhaustion experienced by Emergency Medical Technicians in New York City. Another article focused on the gut-wrenching decision facing a school superintendent in Nevada. He is well aware that being in the classroom is crucial for the students in his poor district, and the governor is encouraging schools to reopen by cutting funding to those that don't. But three teachers in his district recently became ill—and one died—after collaborating on a virtual summer school. I could feel the superintendent's angst. After reading for a while, a heaviness seemed to descend on me. I certainly wasn't happy. But was joy anywhere to be found?

Happiness and joy have much in common, but joy runs deeper, and is anchored in God's character and promises. I picture it this way: Happiness is easily affected by shifting circumstances, the way a body of water reflects the changing weather. On a lovely day the surface is calm and reflects the blue sky, while on a stormy day the water looks grey and choppy. Joy, however, abides deep down, unaffected by storm winds.

Recently, I listened to a recording of *The Book of Joy*, featuring conversations between His Holiness the Dalai Lama and Archbishop Desmond Tutu. Gladness and delight nearly jumped out of the car speakers. And yet, these were men who had lived through serious hardship. The Dalai Lama fled his homeland, which involved a dangerous three-week journey over the mountains, and he has been in exile ever since. Archbishop Tutu went through a period of time when he received frequent death threats. I can't imagine how unnerving that would be. At the time the book was written, he was battling cancer. It was clear, however, that both men faced each day with the attitude that life is a gift. They maintained a sense of humor. These men found that focusing on others brought joy into their own lives.

Philippians 4:4 comes to mind, in which Paul wrote, "Be joyful always. Again, I will say, rejoice." *Always?* Honestly, I want to say, "Come on, Paul, get real!" But wait, he was not writing blithely from a position of ease and comfort. This was a man who had endured beatings, a stoning, and three shipwrecks (2 Cor 11:25)! Paul was also imprisoned several times, and I'm sure he was able to experience the joy of God's presence, even in prison.

Joy is of God and is part of God's character. Consider the following:

God the Father takes joy in his people.

> For the LORD your God is living among you. He is a mighty savior. He will take delight in you with gladness. With his love, he will calm all your fears. He will rejoice over you with joyful songs (Zeph 3:17 NLT).

Jesus had joy, despite knowing that his earthly life would lead to suffering on a cross.

> You have loved righteousness and hated wickedness;
> therefore God, our God, has set you above your compan-
> ions by anointing you with the oil of joy (Heb 1:9; Ps 45:7).

Jesus also promised to share his joy with those who follow
him.

> I have told you this so that my joy may be in you and that
> your joy may be complete (John 15:11).

The Spirit brings forth joy.

> But the fruit of the spirit is love, joy, peace . . . (Gal 5:22)

If indeed joy is of God, and is an attribute of his, it follows that
relationship with God is the source of joy. As King David wrote,
"You make known to me the path of life; you will fill me with joy in
your presence" (Ps 16:11).

There is a strong connection between joy and gratitude.
When we find one, we will find the other. Being joyful leads us
to gratitude, and being thankful helps us discover joy. Even the
words are connected. Pardon me for being a bit of a word nerd, but
you may find this interesting. The Greek word for thanksgiving is
eucharisteo. Within *eucharisteo*, we find *charis*, meaning "grace."
And from *charis*, we get *chara*, meaning "joy."

Keeping a joy journal can be an effective way to get in the habit
of seeing life as a gift, and receiving it with delight. This is similar to
the previously-mentioned gratitude journal. The idea is to simply jot
down things that make your heart smile. A fun variation on this can
be to take photos. Anyone can do this, starting with simple, everyday moments. Here's a list I wrote as I sat on my back deck recently:

- A fresh, hot cup of coffee or tea.

- The warmth of the sun on my skin, or the gentle kiss of snow-
  flakes on my cheek.

- Flowering plants and the leaves of the trees fluttering in the
  breeze.

~ Our companions on this earthly journey: human friends, beloved pets, chirping birds, and the tiny green frog under my chair.

As our practice of joy and gratitude continues, our lists can become more profound. Here's my short list of what I believe to be the greatest sources of joy:

~ God sees us and knows us.

~ God loves us and offers forgiveness.

~ Although there are skirmishes we will fight, Jesus has already won the battle.

These truths can ground our lives, allowing us to rejoice even in the tough times.

Some people hold back from embracing joy out of fear that something bad will happen and the joy won't last. To be sure, life is uncertain and nothing on earth lasts forever. But this is where faith comes in. We do not face the future alone. God will never desert his people. And finally, when all the joys and the struggles of this life are over, a bright future awaits.

I find my mind drifting back to the idea of the beach ball. If someone is worried that the ball will catch the wind, blow into the water, and get carried out to sea, that certainly would dampen the fun of playing with it. We have no guarantee that the beach ball will always have a safe place to land. But consider this—in God, *we* always have a safe place to land. When we trust God with our tomorrows, we can focus on, and celebrate, today's joys. As my father used to remind me, "Keep your eye on the ball."

For our ending prayer, I would like to take these words of Paul and pray them over you, my dear readers.

"May the God of hope fill you with all joy and peace as you trust in him, so that you may overflow with hope by the power of the Holy Spirit." Amen.
ROMANS 15:13

CHAPTER 12—DIVING DEEPER

REFLECT

1. Think about those things that bring you joy and how you can incorporate more of them into your life. If you're not sure, consider:

   + Is time in nature restorative for you?

   + Do you crave time alone, or need companionship?

   + Does cooking engage your senses, focus your mind on the present, and give a sense of control when life feels chaotic?

   + Are singing and dancing expressions of joy for you? On the harder days, are they therapeutic, helping you to find joy?

2. What blocks joy for you?

   + Do guilt, resentment, or unforgiveness keep you chained to the past?

   + Does legalism cause you to turn God's life-giving instructions into a burden?

   + Does envy keep you from appreciating the blessings you have, and from using the gifts you have been given?

   + Does exhaustion zap your joy? (If so, take a nap, then re-read chapter 8—Beach Chair!)

GIVE THANKS

What has given you joy this week? Thank God for those things.

Which of God's promises bring joy to your heart? Tell God what they mean to you.

READ

> You make known to me the path of life;
> You will fill me with joy in your presence,
> With eternal pleasures at your right hand. (Ps 16:11)

Eccl 2:24–25; Deut 16:14; Phil 4:4–8—Gratitude and joy

Rom 12:12—Joy in hope

Ps 5:11; 28:7; 63:7–8—Joy in trust

Isa 49:13; Ps 94:19—Compassion and consolation

Isa 12:1–6—God of salvation

Hab 3:17–18; 1 Pet 1:3–9—Rejoice in hard times

ACT

Implement a plan to incorporate more of what brings joy into your days, remembering to focus on what is doable in your situation.

If you'd like, start a joy journal.

Part III

Stormy Weather

Chapter 13

INTO THE STORM

Do not fear, for I have redeemed you; I have summoned you by name; you are mine. When you pass through the waters, I will be with you; and when you pass through the rivers, they will not sweep over you.

ISAIAH 43:1-2

SUNNY DAYS BY THE WATER can be wonderful. If you're feeling energetic, you can build a sandcastle, swim, surf, bike down the beach, or go sailing. A sunny beach is also a nice place to just plain relax. But the weather isn't always mild, and when a fierce storm blows in, a beach is exposed to the full brunt of its fury.

Our lives aren't always sunny, either. Longfellow famously wrote, "Into each life some rain must fall."* Well, sometimes it's just a little rain—and sometimes it's a full-on hurricane. There are many types of life storms: emergencies, illnesses, accidents, relationship struggles, unemployment—the list goes on. We may see clouds building on the horizon of our lives, or we may be taken by surprise when the phone rings in the middle of the night. Sometimes a squall hits and then is gone as quickly as it came.

---

* Longfellow, "The Rainy Day," in *Complete Poetical Works*, 17.

Other times, clouds stall overhead until we are drenched in tears. Regardless of the warning or the duration, we can be sure storms will come.

While working on final rewrites of this chapter, I received a call informing me that my frail mother had taken a bad fall and was being brought to the ER. The next day, there was a heart-wrenching decision to be made: whether to put her through a lengthy surgery or not. The prognosis was not good either way. It felt like I was in shock. To compound matters, Mom was unable to express her wishes, and it took my brother and me quite a while to reach agreement. As I sat in my mother's hospital room, I pondered this chapter. My first question was rhetorical: *Was it really necessary for me to live through another example of the storms I was writing about?* Then, I wondered which of my own words I would need to put into practice.

Over the course of Mom's hospital stay, the topic that kept coming to mind was self-care. In the midst of a squall, it can be easy to overlook our most basic needs. And yet, we still need water, nourishment and rest. Without them, we can quickly become stressed out and exhausted.

When storms come, we may feel alone, afraid, and unprepared for the battle. How adroitly we handle adverse weather—and our ability to assist others—depends largely on what we have learned from previous experiences, and what resources we have at hand. Were you picturing a blue-sky day as you packed your beach bag? What if the winds howl and the waves threaten? Let's revisit some of the topics we have covered, and the items we packed, in light of this new and turbulent reality.

As we began this book, we noted how essential water is for sustaining life. Food is also vital. In addition to strengthening the body, sometimes food and drink nourish the soul. A bowl of hot soup, or a cup of tea with a friend, can be comforting. In the "Beach Chair" chapter, we looked at the need for rest for our bodies and also for our minds. It can be restorative to just sit in your favorite corner with a warm afghan (or near a cool fan, depending on the season) and allow yourself to relax and just breathe. In my case, after days of weighing the options regarding my mother's treatment, and continuing to mull it over even after the decision was made, I finally gave myself permission to sit down for fifteen minutes and read a book. What a gift it was to think about something else for a little while! I know I was better able to face the continuing challenges after that short mental vacation.

The simple pleasures of food, drink, and rest help us recharge. We can also support others who are having a tough time by bringing food and drink, and encouraging rest, as God's angel did for Elijah.

In the chapter "Beach Creatures" we celebrated the uniqueness of each individual. Every personality type has strengths as well as weaknesses, and reacts to stress in a distinct way. Some people want loved ones around them, while others just want to be left alone. If you were caught in wild weather, would you want to have someone with you? I can think of many times when the caring presence of a friend helped me get through difficult times. Rich Melheim, the energetic pastor who founded Faith Inkubators, speaks of how we put a broken bone in a cast to hold it. He draws the following parallel: when our hearts are broken or our dreams are broken, we need to trust God and our family of faith to hold us while we heal.

Sometimes, when people are caught together in the same storm, the stress everyone experiences can tear relationships and communities apart. To avoid this, being aware of our own needs and those of others is a good place to start. Then, a conscious effort can be made to help and support each other instead of taking our frustrations out on one another.

Do you remember a very small—but important—item we brought along? We put lip balm in our beach bags. This is also helpful in blustery weather, since wind can be as drying as sunshine. As you may recall, this item represents the words we speak. We can get through difficulties more easily when our speech offers grace and kindness to others—and when we are gentle with ourselves.

Before leaving for the beach, we also grabbed sunglasses. While we probably won't be needing to wear them in a storm, the concepts of perception, viewpoint, focal point, and the eyes of faith are crucial. Let's see how these applied when Jesus's disciples got caught in high winds and rough seas. (You can find this story in Matthew 14.)

One evening, Jesus had sent his disciples on ahead in a boat. During the night, the wind came up while the little boat was far out on the water. It was barely able to make any headway against the wind and waves. Then Jesus came walking across the water toward the boat! Instead of sighing with relief, the disciples were terrified. In the darkness, they thought they were seeing a ghost. Jesus spoke reassuringly to them and, at his invitation, Peter decided to get out of the boat and walk over to him. I imagine that Peter was looking to Jesus as he took his first steps on the water. Then, he lost his focus. Matthew tells us, "But when he saw the wind, he was afraid and, beginning to sink, cried out, 'Lord, save me!'" (v. 30). As Peter shouted, his gaze likely returned to Jesus, who immediately "reached out his hand and caught him" (v. 31). Once Jesus and Peter got into the boat, the wind calmed down.

I love that Jesus never told Peter, "Don't think about the wind. Don't look at the waves." Trying *not* to think about something often makes us think about it even more. However, we can use the eyes of faith and redirect our minds to focus on the one who can simply walk across those waves, whose outstretched hand saves us, and whose loving presence calms the storm.

Boating has a lot to teach us about navigating life's storms. Remember when we slipped on our flip-flops and considered simplicity as we chose what to bring with us? If the water gets rough, excess items may end up rolling around the deck, where passengers and crew can trip over them. In a severe storm, even what started out as precious cargo quickly becomes dangerous, excess weight. Likewise, in life, what seemed a reasonable load to carry under normal circumstances might need to be reevaluated in difficult times.

Ideally, boats find a safe harbor before wild weather arrives. But if caught in open waters, the first thing sailors do—before the full force of the wind hits—is reef the sails. This involves tying them in such a way that less area is exposed to the wind. The risk of tearing the sails or damaging the boat is greatly reduced, while still allowing some control. In a similar manner, when our lives are buffeted by storms and high winds, it can be helpful to look for ways to lessen our exposure to that which wears us down. For example, if you have dealt with a crisis all day, perhaps you can skip an evening meeting and relax at home. Life storms may be out of our control, but we do have some choice about conserving our energy elsewhere.

In rough seas, we are more likely to turn to God in prayer than when life is smooth sailing. (As Mike in my writing group said, "There are no atheists on sinking ships.") And yet, it can be hard to pray. Even the most faithful people can feel like God is far away, or might be angry at God for allowing such circumstances. Between the howling winds and our own swirling thoughts, it can be difficult to be receptive to the varied ways God may be trying to communicate with us. It's OK to honestly pour out our hearts to a loving Father, and ask for help to see and hear him. We can also ask our friends to join with us in prayer.

The good book we put in our beach bags will be indispensable. In reading Scripture, we see that almost every person who walked through its pages endured tough times. Often it seems the struggles they faced and the lessons they learned were an inextricable part of their calling. From their examples, we can learn what to do—and what not to do! Meanwhile, the promises we find will help us keep our heads above the waves.

The last item we packed was a beach ball, representing joy. During high winds, we may feel that even the possibility of joy has blown away, just as a beach ball might. But making the effort to find those moments of joy—and being grateful for them—helps us get through the tough times. Let me illustrate this with a story:

Several years ago, my mother suffered spinal fractures and spent a few months in a rehabilitation facility. It was awful to hear her moaning in agony day after day. I advocated for more pain medication. However, when she got it, she became delusional and started calling me at all hours, upset about imaginary problems. Finally, medications were adjusted and she began to heal. Then, prior to discharge, Mom was adamant about returning to her former residence, while the medical staff and I questioned the wisdom and safety of that. There were intense exchanges before we came to an agreement. To sum things up, those months in rehab were awful for Mom, and they also took a toll on me. Yet, they were not without any spark of joy.

One day as I walked out of the facility, I took a moment to just enjoy the beauty of the autumn day. Oak trees surrounded the parking lot. Looking down, I saw the pavement was absolutely covered with acorns—such cute little things, with their tiny beanies on top! Pausing to admire them, I pictured squirrels gathering them in the woods. Then I got a bag out of the car and began to gather them myself. To me, they were tiny, free gifts. Little joys. I brought them home and smiled as I displayed them in the front hall, where everyone coming in could enjoy them. Now, every fall, acorns remind me to be alert for little moments of joy in life, especially when joy seems hard to find—for that is when we need it the most.

As I wrote the first two sections of this book, I was primarily thinking of a calm and pleasant day by the shore, and that's probably what you pictured as you read. However, we now know that when the winds howl and the waves threaten, the items we carefully chose to bring along will be effective storm gear.

So, next time you find yourself in harsh conditions, remember:

- ⁀ Take care of yourself.

- ⁀ Let friends support you.

- ⁀ Offer grace to those around you—and yourself.

- ⁀ Even if salt water sprays in your eyes, strive to keep your perspective.

- Talk with God, inviting the Creator of the seas to help you keep your head above water.
- Allow God's word to encourage your heart.
- Lift your head now and then to look for moments of joy.

Dear Father,
We would rather not face life's strong winds and the immense
waves that threaten to knock us over. Yet, we thank you for the
many ways in which you equip us and walk with us. Thank
you for the example of Jesus, who endured the worst this world
can give, and emerged victorious. Amen.

CHAPTER 13—DIVING DEEPER

REFLECT

1. Think back to a rough time you went through. How did you take care of yourself? Would you approach self-care differently next time?

2. Is there a particular concept or beach bag item that you want to focus on during a current storm, or keep in mind for the future?

3. Reflect on moments when friends or family comforted you. Do these memories elicit ideas for ways to support others in their struggles?

GIVE THANKS

෴ for supportive companions.

෴ for a quiet space to be alone when you need solitude.

෴ for glimpses of beauty, simple comforts, and little moments of laughter.

෴ for the promise of God's abiding presence, in calm weather and in storms.

READ

"We do not know what to do, but our eyes are upon you" (2 Chr 20:12).

Ps 103:13–14; Isa 49:13–17—compassion

Ps 91:14–15—God's presence and deliverance

Ps 107:23–31—safe harbor

John 16:33—peace

ACT

Choose a Bible verse or section to encourage you through a current or future storm. Write it out or, better yet, commit it to memory.

Make a list of simple ways to brighten a dark day for yourself or someone else.

Ask God to open your eyes to someone who could use your understanding and support.

Chapter 14

A Stowaway in the Bag

The wise man in the storm prays God not for safety from
danger but for deliverance from fear.
It is the storm within which endangers him
not the storm without.

RALPH WALDO EMERSON

When I was growing up, my family took trips on our boat and
we occasionally got into some rough waters. Once, we were sitting on the flying bridge above the main deck, bouncing through
the waves, when we heard clunking noises down below. I quickly
descended the ladder to check it out, and will never forget the sight
as I entered the main cabin. Our little dog was cowering under
the couch while our cooking pots rolled around the floor! The
movement of the boat in the rough water must have jostled them
enough to push open the cabinet door and he was terrified. Like
that dog, when we encounter storms in our lives, whether literal
or metaphorical, often our first response is fear. No matter how
intentional we were about packing our bags, we are likely to realize
that we are carrying fear along with us, too.

Fear is a powerful force. It is protective, often motivating us
to make life-saving choices. It drives those in the path of a fire or

storm to evacuate while they can. But fear is destructive if we let it take over. In fact, fear can be the breeding ground for evil. Fears of loss, of change, of those who are different, and of what we do not understand, have led to some of history's darkest chapters.

God knows that many situations cause us to be frightened. When people have encounters with the divine, "Be not afraid" or "Do not fear" are often the first words spoken by angels and by God. Jesus spoke those words to his disciples. In fact, this is the most frequent injunction in the Bible. Some people say that some version of this message appears in Scripture 365 times. I love the idea of having a quote of God's reassurance for every day of the year!

When events surprise and frighten me, I find comfort in remembering that God is still on the throne of heaven, and nothing which happens today—or tomorrow—surprises him. As Charles Spurgeon declared in his book, *Morning and Evening*, "Away, then, all fears. The kingdom is safe in the King's hands."*

While it's healthy to acknowledge our fears, we do not need to let them run our lives. We can experience fear, and still act with courage. As Franklin D. Roosevelt said, "Courage is not the absence of fear, but rather the assessment that something else is more important than fear."** You could think of that "something" as a fear of a different sort. For example, are we more afraid of speaking up on behalf of someone and being criticized or even attacked, or of remaining silent and regretting it? It is in this context that I would like to mention the fear of the Lord. Fear of the Lord doesn't necessarily mean to quake in our boots, but to trust God and desire to honor him. This is one type of fear Scripture encourages! "The fear of the Lord is the beginning of wisdom" (Prov 9:10; Ps 111:10a). When we fear God, we hold him in such honor that pleasing him is our top priority. "Blessed are those who fear the Lord, who find great delight in his commands" (Ps 112:1).

---

* Spurgeon, *Morning & Evening*, 414.

** The History Hour, *Franklin Delano Roosevelt*, epigraph.

WORRY AND ANXIETY

When we have concerns, it is wise to pray and seek constructive solutions. As Proverbs 22:3 states, "The prudent see danger and take refuge, but the simple keep going and pay the penalty." However, when we *worry*, we get stuck in our concerns and difficulties, and let those thoughts pitch a tent in our minds. The derivation of the word *worry* goes back to Old English, and can be used for a dog chewing on a bone. This is a helpful picture. Grasp, tug, gnaw—we keep chewing on it, but don't really get anywhere. As Jesus said, "Can any one of you by worrying add a single hour to your life?" (Matt 6:27).

We all go through stressful times, but there is a difference between occasionally feeling anxious and clinical anxiety. If you, dear reader, are dealing with the latter, my heart goes out to you. Someone very near and dear to me suffers from an anxiety disorder. Over the years, I have tried to speak words of comfort and reassurance into her life, and her response is usually, "I *know* that, but it doesn't help." I understand what she means. There have been times in my life when I have experienced a level of anxiety that tied my stomach in knots. Those knots were slow to loosen, regardless of what my mind, or even Scripture, said. If you relate to this, be gentle on yourself. Do not add guilt or condemnation to the struggles you already have. I hope this chapter encourages you and gives you Scriptures to help set your thoughts on a firm foundation, even while you wrestle with feelings of anxiety. As with clinical depression, you cannot simply talk your way out of anxiety. A medical doctor or mental health professional may be able to give you further assistance.

COPING STRATEGIES

As we discussed in the previous chapter, focusing on trying *not* to be worried, anxious, or afraid isn't very effective. Our brains respond much better when we tell them what *to* do. Here are some strategies:

1. Acknowledge your fears. You can pray about them, talk them out with an understanding friend, and/or journal. Then picture leaving the weight of them with the Lord, in the care of your friend, or on the pages of your journal.

2. Focus on God and "seek first his kingdom" (Matt 6:33). Spend time with him. You can't trust someone you don't know. Read his word. Take your time and let it soak into your heart and soul. The Diving Deeper section suggests helpful passages.

3. Be good to yourself. Fear, worry, and anxiety are exhausting. Check in with your body and relax areas where you are holding tension. Practice self-care and enjoy some fresh air and exercise.

4. Think and pray about whether there is some action you can take. For example, when my first child was a newborn, a fear of Sudden Infant Death Syndrome (SIDS) lodged in my severely sleep-deprived brain. I made a donation to the American SIDS Institute. Although I knew it wouldn't directly make a difference for my baby, being able to do *something*, and knowing it would help others in the future, made me feel better.

5. Look for small miracles and points of gratitude.

6. Laughter is a great antidote to fear. If the concern is not deadly serious, see if you can catastrophize to the point of ridiculousness. For example, one of my young music students was apprehensive about an upcoming recital and asked what would happen if he made a mistake.

    I responded, "The roof will collapse, your parents will leave without you, and I won't teach you anymore."

    He looked at me intently for a moment before a grin spread across his face. "That won't happen."

    I smiled reassuringly. "No, it won't," I said, and we both chuckled.

7. If you are concerned about certain events which are getting news coverage, limit your exposure to the media. TV, in particular, tends to sensationalize issues. Don't let your brain marinate in that negativity!

8. Jesus advised, "Therefore do not worry about tomorrow . . . Each day has enough trouble of its own" (Matt 6:34). Jesus was not saying we should never think about the future, but that we would do well to concentrate on what we need to do today. Years ago, during an unsettling time in my life, my mantra became "One day at a time." It really helped me focus on dealing with what each day presented—without stressing over things that *could* happen or decisions that *might* need to be made.

NEVER ALONE

Instead of a debilitating load of fear, worry, and anxiety, there is one biblical truth that God's people can carry with them. I'd like to illustrate it with this story from my trip to Israel.

Our small group was at Masada, the site of Herod's winter palace, and a place he could escape to if under threat. It was also the scene of the dramatic last stand of the Jews against the Roman Empire after the fall of Jerusalem. The topography of the place is what allowed it to be both a place of escape and a rebel stronghold. Masada sits on the flat top of a rocky mesa, approximately 1,500 feet above the Dead Sea. The original path to the top was called "The Snake Path." As the name suggests, it was a treacherous climb.

One of the people in our tour group had acrophobia, the fear of heights. She braved the gondola which now takes visitors most of the way up to the top. We climbed a little higher and toured the ruins. However, as we headed back down the path along the sheer edge of the mesa towards where we could catch the gondola, fear gripped her. Finally, unable to summon the courage to take one more step, she froze, saying "I can't." Well, leaving her there on the edge of the cliff was really not an option! Our guide went and stood beside her, taking his place on the outside edge of the path. His presence helped block her view of the terrifying drop. He spoke reassuringly, and she could sense his calm confidence. He then walked with her, step-by-step, back to the gondola, which carried her to the security of the valley floor. This is exactly what our God has promised to do for God's people. There is no promise we will never be in frightening situations, but God does promise to be with us. The more we focus on God's presence, the less we focus on what frightens us.

King David wrote, "Even though I walk through the darkest valley I will fear no evil, for you are with me . . . " (Ps 23:4a).

King Jesus told his disciples, "And be sure of this: I am with you always, even to the end of the age" (Matt 28:20b).

Our Father and King gave this assurance: "So do not fear, for I am with you; do not be dismayed, for I am your God. I will strengthen you and help you; I will uphold you with my righteous right hand" (Isa 41:10).

PEACE

As we trade our fear for trust, and focus on God's presence, we can begin to experience God's peace. "You will keep in perfect peace those whose minds are steadfast, because they trust in you" (Isa 26:3). The English word "peace" cannot begin to contain all the meaning of the Hebrew concept of *shalom*. Shalom means peace, wholeness, everything as it should be. God promises God's own peace to his children, even when all around seems to be chaos.

Remember, my friends, we may not be *fearless*, but we can certainly learn to *fear less*.

Dear Lord,
Sometimes this world is a scary place. We are afraid when
events remind us of past traumas, and we are unnerved when
circumstances are totally unfamiliar. Even in the midst of the
storm, help us to hear your voice saying, "Do not fear, for I am
with you."
Amen.

CHAPTER 14—DIVING DEEPER

REFLECT

1. What scares you the most?

2. Are there issues in which you tend to cross the line from prayerful, constructive problem-solving into just plain fretting?

3. Which of the coping strategies are you already doing? Which would you like to try?

4. Remember God's faithfulness to his people, and to you, through past storms. If you keep a journal, looking through it can jog your memory.

GIVE THANKS

↩ for God's enduring love and faithfulness.

↩ for simple comforts (the sun on your shoulder, a cup of tea, a cozy place to rest).

↩ for the people who are offering you their love and support.

READ

For I am the LORD, your God, who takes hold of your right hand and says to you, 'Do not fear; I will help you' (Isa 41:13).

Matt 6:25–33—worry

1 Pet 5:7; Phil 4:6–8—anxiety

Isa 33:6; 35:3–4—fear of the Lord

Ps 46:1–3; Isa 44:1–2; 2 Chr 20:1–30—fear

Ps 23:4; 46:1–3; 73:23–26—never alone

Ps 4:8; 29:11; John 14:27; 16:33; Isa 54:10—peace

ACT

Implement whichever coping strategies you think will be most helpful.

Provide encouragement to someone who is afraid. It may be through your presence, your prayers, or some other way.

Choose a Scripture passage from this chapter that spoke to your heart. Handwrite it or type it with a favorite font. If you feel inspired, use a calligraphy pen or decorate it with artwork. Hang it where you will see it. Memorize it, so it is always with you.

Chapter 15

WAVES OF DOUBT

If you desire faith, then you have faith enough.

ELIZABETH BARRETT BROWNING

HAVE YOU EVER STOOD shin-deep in the ocean, with the waves breaking close by? In case you haven't, let me tell you what it's like. As the water recedes, you feel a strong pull. The sea seems to want to take both you and part of the beach with it. The sand around, and under, your feet is suddenly washed away and you are left struggling to retain your balance. That's how doubting can feel.

If doubting frightens you because you feel as if the foundation is being pulled away, that actually says something positive about your faith. It shows you are building your life on God's word. Someone who keeps God at a distance isn't going to care as much about doubts, or seek as hard to find answers.

When you find yourself struggling with doubts and questions, don't panic. You are not alone! In fact, you're in very good company. I found it oddly comforting when I learned Mother Theresa sometimes had serious doubts about God. This month, I have been taking a fascinating class from Rabbi Shai Held, who reads biblical Hebrew like it's his native language, has a profound knowledge of Scripture, and offers rich insights. I was surprised—and taken with his honesty—when he casually began a sentence with the words, "On the days I still believe in God . . . " The pages of Scripture, too, are full of characters who grappled with deep uncertainty at times, and even wrestled with God.

It is human nature to believe what we see (even though we know pictures can be Photoshopped and our eyes can trick us), and question what we cannot see. But this gets turned upside down when Paul tells us, "Now faith is confidence in what we hope for and assurance about what we do not see" (Heb 11:1). And: "We live by faith, not by sight" (1 Cor 5:6–9). As mere mortals, it is difficult for us to wrap our minds around the very concept of an eternal God who is Spirit. It's no wonder that we don't always understand his ways, and sometimes question his very existence. The prophet Isaiah plainly tells us, "'For my thoughts are not your thoughts, neither are your ways my ways,' declares the LORD. 'As the heavens are higher than the earth, so are my ways higher than your ways and my thoughts than your thoughts'" (Isa 55:8–9). If we could plainly see and completely understand God, would he be a holy God, worthy of our worship?

The funny thing is that while at times I may question God's existence, I know that if I tried to be an atheist, I'd have my doubts about that, too. Besides, I think simply believing that God exists is somewhat overrated anyway. After all, Scripture says that the devil believes and trembles (Jas 2:19). True faith is not so much about believing *in* God as it is BELIEVING GOD —trusting him!

Instead of thinking of doubts as fighting against my faith, I find doubts are less of a struggle when I can think of them as somehow *part of* my faith. Even in close human relationships, when we can plainly see and hear each other, there are times we do not understand why the other person did or said something, or why he/she failed to do so. We may have times when we feel unloved and disconnected. Those struggles are part of the relationship. And if human relationships involve questions and struggles, should we be surprised that a relationship with a holy God is challenging?

If you've ever tried to muster up more faith, you have probably found it can't be done. Actually, the Bible states that faith is a gift from God. In his first letter to the church at Corinth, Paul writes about the variety of gifts that God bestows on his people. Not everyone gets the same ones in the same quantity. And faith is one of those gifts (1 Cor 12:4–11). Paul even says faith is "the gift of God . . . so that no one can boast" (Eph 2:8, 10). Doubts do help keep us humble about our walk with God. (By the way, in the unlikely event that anyone reading this chapter is wondering what a doubt is because you've never had one: don't look down on us doubters, and do thank God for your faith!)

Sometimes we forget that as human beings, when we are tired, sick, or emotionally out of sorts, it can affect us in a variety of ways. I've noticed that when I'm feeling down, I'm more inclined to doubt my own abilities and question how much those around me care. I'm also more prone to doubting God. Perhaps it's not a crisis of faith so much as a sign that it's time to take better care of myself!

While doubts and questions can be very unsettling, they are not all bad. Questioning is part of finding our way. Even for those who have had the blessing of being raised in a godly family, no one can simply appropriate someone else's beliefs. We need to make them our own. As we raise questions, we may reach new understandings. Doubt can serve to challenge our faith, keeping it from getting stagnant. We may, in the end, develop deeper convictions.

I have always been a bit of a skeptic and used to joke that "Thomas the Doubter" was my patron saint. You may know Thomas's story. The disciples were meeting together when the resurrected Jesus appeared to them. But Thomas wasn't with them. When the others told Thomas they'd seen the Lord, he responded, "Unless I see the nail marks in his hands and put my finger where the nails were, and put my hand into his side, I will not believe" (John 20:25b). A friend recently commented that she thought poor Thomas has gotten a bad rap. Perhaps he was simply trying to follow Jesus' instructions. After all, Jesus had previously warned the disciples, "Watch out that no one deceives you. Many will come in my name, claiming, 'I am he,' and will deceive many" (Mark 13:5–6). Sometimes a little skepticism is healthy!

Regardless of the root cause of Thomas's doubts, I love how this story ends. Jesus comes to the disciples again, and this time, despite his uncertainty, Thomas is with them. Jesus offers Thomas exactly what he requested. "Put your finger here; see my hands. Reach out your hand and put it into my side. Stop doubting and believe." Thomas makes a confession of faith. And here's the best part: "Then Jesus told him, "Because you have seen me, you have believed; blessed are those who have not seen and yet have believed" (John 10:27, 29). Wait—did you catch that? It's almost as if Jesus turned from Thomas to directly address us. We haven't seen Jesus during his ministry on earth. We haven't heard his audible, human voice. He knew it wouldn't be easy for us to believe and he pronounced a blessing on us.

So, what can we do when we don't feel "faith-full?"

✦ *Honestly bring questions to God.* It's good to know that God is not threatened or intimidated by our doubts. He knows what we're thinking anyway, so there's no use pretending. Honest questions are part of seeking to know him. Let's ask God to grant us wisdom and understanding, and patience as we learn. I think it's safe to say everyone has heard of Abraham, Isaac, and Jacob. There's an interesting story about Jacob in Genesis. At a crucial moment in his life, he encountered God and was given a new name: Israel. And what is the meaning of that name? "He who wrestles with God." In our doubts and questions, let's wrestle well. (But do keep in mind, as Job learned, the Almighty One *owes* you no explanations.)

✦ *Stay in the word.* Sometimes a passage just doesn't sit right with us, and we want to stop reading. But don't give up. Keep reading. Keep learning. Be sure to consider passages in their context, and when a section confuses you, check how your understanding lines up with other Scripture passages on the subject. I find that the more I learn about biblical context, original language, the teaching style of first-century rabbis, etc., the better I can grasp how the first hearers or readers would have understood it. Some rough passages have become clearer. However, if anyone said he/she has never wrestled with the meaning of Scripture, I would question how much they have actually read!

- *Stay in fellowship.* Let's follow the example of the disciples, shortly after Jesus' death. They had not understood everything Jesus had said, and now he was gone. They were confused, disillusioned, and frightened. But they were *together*, seeking comfort and understanding, and Jesus came to them. During times of doubt, it can be tempting to avoid fellowship. However, when we do, we are cutting off avenues by which God can come to us and meet us in our doubts and questionings.

- *Remember.* Remembering how God has blessed us and carried us through the tough times can give us strength for the present and hope for the future. We often do not understand what God is doing in the moment, but when we look back, we more clearly see his hand. Throughout Scripture we read, "Write these words," "Read these words," and "Teach them to your children," so that we—and they—remember. God wants us to remember the stories in Scripture of divine mercy and faithfulness. And God wants us to remember the mercy and faithfulness we have been shown. As I mentioned in chapter 9, some people keep a journal as a way to record and remember how God has taught them, walked with them, and answered prayers. If you keep one, take some time to read it when you need a little boost to your faith. If you don't keep a journal, you might consider starting one.

One thing to avoid when we're having doubts—or any other time, for that matter—is comparing ourselves, and our faith journey, to others. When I was young, someone told me that if I invited Jesus into my life, I could sit in the car and talk to him, and he'd answer just as if he was sitting beside me. Well, that may have been her experience, but it has not been mine and for years that troubled me. There have been other instances, too, in which I have doubted God and/or wondered what was wrong with me, because my experience didn't match up to someone else's. Each person is unique and God meets us in different ways.

In times of doubt, let's remind one another that while our faith may be weak, God is strong. *Ultimately, our trust is not in our own ability to hang on to God, but in his ability to hang onto us.* Like the father of the boy whom Jesus healed, we can pray "I do believe; help me overcome my unbelief" (Mark 9:24). After all, Jesus is "the pioneer and perfecter of faith," not we ourselves (Heb 12:2).

Even a little faith can grow and be used by God to accomplish great things. We may have doubts and questions, but we can walk in the light we do have. "And I am sure that he who began a good work in you will bring it to completion at the day of Jesus Christ" (Phil 1:6 RSV).

Our ending prayer comes from the hymn, "We Walk by Faith."

> *Help then, O Lord, our unbelief;*
> *And may our faith abound,*
> *To call on thee when thou art near,*
> *And seek where thou art found:*
> *That, when our life of faith is done,*
> *In realms of clearer light*
> *We may behold thee as thou art,*
> *With full and endless sight.**
> *Amen.*

* Text: Henry Alford, 1810–1871, alt.

CHAPTER 15—DIVING DEEPER

REFLECT

1. What ideas in this chapter were most helpful to you?

2. This chapter began with the opening quote, "If you desire faith, then you have faith enough." Do you agree or disagree? Why?

3. We read about remembering. Is there a particular time or incident in your life when God's presence and power were so clear that the memory serves as a touchstone? Journal about that and/or share it with your group.

4. Do you think there is a difference between doubt and unbelief?

Consider the following quote:

> Christ never failed to distinguish between doubt and unbelief. Doubt is *"can't believe."* Unbelief is *"won't believe."* Doubt is honesty. Unbelief is obstinacy. Doubt is looking for light. Unbelief is content with darkness.**

GIVE THANKS

Thank God that he holds his children fast. (John 10:27–29 "No one can snatch them out of my hand.")

Thank Jesus for his patience. After all, he put up with—and loved—the original twelve doubting, and often clueless, disciples!

** Drummond, *Greatest Thing*, 113 (emphasis original).

READ

Why are you downcast, O my soul? Why so disturbed within me? Put your hope in God, for I will yet praise him, my Savior and my God (Ps 42:11).

John 20:24–29—Jesus meets Thomas in his doubts

ACT

Take inventory. How do you feel in general at the times you are doubting? If you are tired and worn down, do you think a little more self-care would make a difference? If so, make plans for that.

Have an honest conversation with your Heavenly Father about your doubts and questions.

It's tempting to pull away from fellowship when we doubt. Instead, surround yourself with people who can accept you, doubts and all, and can support your faith.

Chapter 16

BOUNDARIES

Draw your boundary lines with a pen of compassion.

J.B. HAZELTON

THERE ARE MANY DIFFERENT types of beaches, all encompassed in one definition: a beach is the boundary between land and water. Sometimes I like to stand right at the water's edge, where the sand is wet and the water tickles my toes. At the ocean, my dog loves to run and play at the edge of the surf, too. What fun! But boundaries are serious business.

When the water recedes below expected levels, bays turn to mud and boats run aground. Worse yet is the destruction that occurs when water levels rise and overrun the usual boundary with the land. Think of the devastation wrought by tsunamis and major storms. In the days after superstorm Sandy hit the US, I read a crazy story. In one of New Jersey's coastal towns, a resident looked out the window at his flooded back yard. There was a shark splashing about! Neither the sea nor its creatures were staying where they belonged.

Boundaries are important at the beach—and also in our lives. Personal boundaries promote health, happiness, and peaceful co-existence with others. Each of us can draw a line around ourselves and ask others to respect that. However, these border lines cannot control others. We decide what *we* will do if that line is not respected, and provide our own border patrol. It is better to safeguard what is within our own borders than to allow others to trample on us and then become angry with them. If we pretend things are fine when they aren't, we can doom a relationship to a slow death by resentment. Ultimately, if limits are continually ignored, we may need to extricate ourselves from a particular situation or put distance in a relationship.

Have you heard the saying, "Never put your key to happiness in someone else's pocket"? Whoever wrote this knew something it took me years to learn: I was too easily handing over responsibilities that fell within my borders. Here's an example. In the first years of my marriage, I remember going on long car trips with my husband. He was in the driver's seat—literally. I told him when I got hungry, expecting him to stop so I could get a lunch or snack. Instead, he usually responded, "Well, we're going to stop for dinner in two or three hours." He has a different metabolism than I do and can easily skip a meal. But when I'm hungry, I'm *hungry*, and I don't want to wait a few hours. He wasn't taking care of me as I expected. Feeling hurt and unloved (as well as hungry), I dropped the subject. Years later I realized I did not need to give him the job of making sure I got fed. My nutritional needs were my responsibility! I could pack snacks. Or I could state my needs more clearly, such as: "my personal fuel tank is running low and I need to fill up at the next town." I'm sure that would have solved the problem.

Boundary-setting can be done with kindness and perhaps even a touch of humor. Let's say you have a friend who calls you earlier in the morning than you like. You have the choice of continuing to be annoyed by the early morning calls, ignoring the phone and feeling guilty, or speaking up. You could say something like, "Susan, I really love our morning chats. *And* I need my sleep. Let's try to talk after 8:30." Or, "Dan, I admire that you are so cheerful and energetic in the morning. However, I'm not a morning person. In fact, my family jokes about steering clear until I've had my morning coffee. How about if I call you a little later, when I'm more awake?"

In chapter 10, "Lip Balm," we considered the power of words. Sometimes, in order to protect ourselves, it is necessary to draw boundaries around what type of communication we will tolerate. While we cannot dictate what others do or don't say, we can choose how we respond, or whether we are going to hang around and listen. This requires discernment. If someone is clearly setting him/herself up as an enemy, it is often wisest and safest to not respond at all. But what about a friend, relative, or coworker who speaks rudely? Let's not fuss over every word people say to us—we all have off days—but when we see a pattern of disrespect, it's time to consider politely speaking up. Are we really doing someone a favor by letting that person think speaking to another person discourteously is OK? If the person is reasonable, we may accomplish three things by gently drawing a line: conserving our emotional energy for what God has called us to do in the world; giving the other person the opportunity to examine his/her behavior and grow; and preventing others from being subjected to the same treatment.

Someone I know used to talk down to me at times as if I was a clueless child. (Yes, I can be absentminded at times, but I am reasonably intelligent.) When I finally confronted this person and let him know how belittled I felt when spoken to that way, the results were amazing. He started giving a little more thought to his words and began treating me with more respect. Often, you don't get what you want until you ask for it!

I have had to learn a lot about boundaries in my life, and am still learning. One thing I now know is that boundaries are easiest to put in place early on, before unhealthy patterns and expectations are established. To use the example from the beginning of this chapter, it's better to keep a shark off your property than to try to remove it once it is swimming in your backyard!

Jesus's followers are called to love and serve others. However, this does not mean putting up with whatever people throw our way and saying yes to every request. How do we balance our own needs and the needs of others? Let's consider what Paul had to say in his letter to the church in Galatia (Galatians 6). Verse 2 reads, "Carry each other's burdens, and in this way you will fulfill the law of Christ." Yet verse 5 says, "for each one should carry his own load." *Wait! What?* At a quick glance, those verses may seem contradictory, because "burden" and "load" are almost interchangeable. However, Paul's point quickly comes into focus when we look at the original Greek.

The actual words Paul used were *baros* and *phortion*. Paul would have been familiar with these terms in reference to the load on a sailing ship. *Baros* (v. 2) means "overloaded." An overloaded ship is in danger of taking on water and sinking. Perhaps Paul, who had been shipwrecked more than once, had learned this the hard way. On the other hand, *phortion* (v. 5) means "a normal load." Not only can a ship safely carry some cargo, a certain amount of weight actually helps it sail well and prevents it from being tossed about in the waves. Paul was saying it's good for each of us to carry our own reasonable load. Each should handle his/her own appropriate responsibilities. However, when someone is overloaded—overwhelmed by life's circumstances—we are called to show God's love by coming alongside to help.

Are God's people called to love, to have compassion, and to serve? Absolutely! Most of us have heard this message loud and clear. However, what we have not always heard is that it's prudent to set boundaries. Think about this: if we allow ourselves to be doormats, constantly stomped on by others, how can we stand up and serve God? When we take responsibility for ourselves and make sure we are nourished in body, soul, and spirit, then we can most fully live out our unique calling.

In establishing healthy boundaries, we can look to the example of Jesus. He showed love by recognizing and responding to people's deepest needs. However, he never lost sight of why he was on Earth, and never let anyone dissuade him from his mission. He felt compassion for the crowds, yet took a break when he and his disciples needed it. He also had the courage to speak the truth, even when it was not what people wanted to hear.

Lord of Creation,
Thank you for drawing boundaries
between the land and the water.
Help us set boundaries that are fair and loving,
so that we and those around us can flourish.
Amen.

CHAPTER 16—DIVING DEEPER

REFLECT

1. Wise King Solomon wrote, "Above all else, guard your heart, for everything you do flows from it" (Prov 4:23). Do you think this advice relates to boundaries? Pray about what "guard your heart" might look like in your life.

2. What did Jesus instruct his disciples to do if they were not welcomed in a town (see Mark 6:11)? Have there been times in your life when the best thing you could do was walk away?

3. When did somebody make a boundary clear to you, and how did that impact your relationship? Consider both the short-term and the long-term affects.

GIVE THANKS

Think of someone in your life who is good at lovingly setting and enforcing boundaries. Thank that person for the example!

READ

You set a boundary [the waters] cannot cross; never again will they cover the earth (Ps 104:9).

Gen 1:9–10; Jer 5:22; Job 38:11—boundaries between land and sea

ACT

When you start to feel angry, or feel like you are being used, ask yourself why. Your feelings may be telling you that you need to set a boundary. When you are calm, choose a gentle way to do that, and an appropriate time.

If you need help establishing reasonable boundaries, consider discussing this with the person whose example you admire (see the "Give Thanks" section above).

Chapter 17

OUT OF THE DARKNESS

He lifted me out of the pit of despair,
out of the mud and the mire.
He set my feet on solid ground and steadied me
as I walked along.

PSALM 40:2 (NLT)

SOMETIMES THE FORCE OF a life storm hits with such severity that it feels as if the flood waters have picked us up, swept us away from the safe and familiar, and left us in a muddy pit. It's a lonely and scary place. We may wonder if God sees us there and cares about our situation. We question if there's any way out. Have you ever felt like that?

In the front of this book (in the Note to Reader), I wrote that healing can be found in the sharing of our stories. Now it's time for me to fully put that into practice, though it is not easy to put my struggles and unwise decisions on these pages for all to read. However, the point of the story is not the details of my storm, but how God was faithful to shine his light into my darkness. My heart's prayer is that sharing this part of my journey will be a source of comfort and hope for you and those around you.

As you may remember, my home is in the Pacific Northwest—more specifically, in the suburbs of Seattle. Our location between the waters and the mountains is spectacularly beautiful, and also gives us a rather unique climate. For most of the year, thick clouds blow in from the coast. As they reach the foothills, they rise, cool, and frequently drizzle or rain on us. In addition, Seattle is as far north as northern Maine, and that latitude makes for short daylight hours in winter. Long before I had heard of Seasonal Affective Disorder (SAD), a type of depression triggered by lack of light, I was aware that my energy and mood both slumped in winter.

My husband and I loved our first home in a wooded neighborhood, but on gloomy winter days I felt like I was in a cave. The darkness doesn't bother my husband, a Northwest native who can't imagine living anywhere else. Since my growing-up years were on the sunnier East Coast, I used to tease him that he just didn't know any better. While he didn't quite understand my struggles, he came to accept that they were real, and asked if a brighter home would help. I jumped at the possibility! Did I dare hope we would find something with a water view, as I had always dreamed of?

We looked at a variety of properties before finding a lovely house that was under construction. It had a view to the foothills and a peek at the lake. This was the one! A meeting was arranged with the realtor and the builder. Just prior to the appointment, I was at home, scrambling to get it ready for sale. The phone rang. It was my husband and his first words were, "You'd better sit down." He had just learned that his employment was not as secure as we'd thought. Our meeting was cancelled, as were plans to buy the house.

Spring and summer had passed by the time my husband found a new job and worked there long enough that a bank would consider giving us a loan. The days began to shorten again. Between the tall trees and the low clouds, I felt claustrophobic. What was weighing on me even more heavily, though, was the fact that my husband and I were in a difficult season of our marriage. One evening, the miscommunication and lack of connection were undeniable. My heart ached. The next morning, as I watched the raindrops run down the windows, tears of despair began to slip down my cheeks. Something had to change. I know I should have gotten on my knees, but I got in my car instead.

I drove a couple miles down the hill, turned along the lake, and soon spotted a for-sale sign. An older home, perched on the hill above the lake, was on the market. I asked our realtor to show it to me. As soon as I saw the charming window seat overlooking the lake, I was smitten. Well, they say love is blind, and I confess I loved the view so much that I glossed over the problem areas of the house. My husband's opinion was that, despite the need for renovations, it was more workable than most lakeview properties in our price range. We decided to buy it, move in, and then plan a remodel.

Our house was put on the market. Shortly after a sale agreement was negotiated, the retail business my husband was working for began rapid expansion. Too rapid. Their budget was stretched to the breaking point and the new controller—my husband—was getting caught in the crossfire. With that stress at work, he was quickly running out of energy and enthusiasm for the major remodeling project that lay ahead. About the same time, I began to feel physically ill. Each morning, after watching my kids get on the school bus, I'd go back inside and lie down. With my insides cramping up, I would think, *I should be packing to move, but right now I don't even want to move off this bed.* Tests soon indicated inflammatory bowel disease. This was not a good time for either of us to sort, pack, relocate, and remodel, but it was too late to turn back.

In December, we took possession of the lakeview house. Before moving in, I brought potpourri to try to banish the musty smell, and hung Christmas lights in an attempt to make it look cheerful. There were daily trips to meet electricians, plumbers, appliance repair people, handymen, etc. By the time moving day arrived, a lot of work had been done, but we were only beginning to realize the extent of what we had gotten ourselves into.

You know the way Snoopy, from the Peanuts gang, begins his novels with: "It was a dark and stormy night?" Well, moving day was dark and stormy. At one point, the movers just stopped, hoping the torrential rain would let up, but it didn't. Then the wind picked up. The lights blinked as the basement furniture was being carried down the stairs. I prayed no one would get hurt and was thankful that the lights stayed on until after the move was complete. Then the power went out. Perhaps this was a portent of the darkness I was entering.

The move had been intended to help me feel better, but I felt worse. While packing up, I had experienced an unusual feeling of loneliness. I now realized those feelings were like the first breezes of an approaching storm. Sleep had become elusive. My doctor prescribed medicine that helped me fall asleep, but I'd be awake again two hours later. In the mornings, I could barely muster the energy to get out of bed and get my kids to school. Normally I have a very healthy appetite, but even when my stomach was growling, food did not interest me. At times, I could not stop the tears. There was no question—I was among the over 16 million Americans who experience clinical depression each year. I would like to say right here that if you, dear reader, fight this battle, know you are not alone, and it is not your fault. Hold on to hope. Take care of yourself with healthful food and exercise (preferably outdoors), and remember that sometimes the wisest and bravest thing you can do is seek help.

In my head, I knew there were far worse problems than mine. But it *felt* like my world was caving in. The feeling was akin to grief, as though someone close to me had died. However, grief tends to come and go in waves, whereas this depression seemed to hover over me at all times, not unlike the Seattle-area clouds in winter.

My mood affected my perception. Much like when wearing sunglasses indoors, everything appeared dark. The only thing I liked was the view, and even that had changed. Gone were the sparkling blue waters of summer. Now, beneath the wintry sky, the lake looked cold, dark, and bleak—just the way I felt. When my daughter wailed, "I want to go hoooome," her words tore at my heart. I could empathize with her—this place did not feel like home. And I felt just awful about my role in her unhappiness. It turns out depression is fertile ground for guilt.

Like many people who battle depression, I also struggled with feeling it was my own fault. I told a doctor that I was really trying to maintain a positive attitude. He looked me straight in the eye and said, "You can't talk your way out of this." That is exactly what I needed to hear. While there are steps an individual can take to help manage symptoms, depression cannot simply be banished with a pep talk. I was reminded that some factors contributing to mood disorders, such as genetics, are out of an individual's control. For those who are susceptible, there are many triggers, including shifting hormones, ongoing stress, and physical illness.

Meanwhile, each day brought new discoveries about the house. Some were merely annoying, such as the time we tried to bake cookies, only to realize that behind the full-size oven door, the actual oven was too small to even fit a cookie sheet. (No Thanksgiving turkey in this oven! A Cornish hen was about all that would fit.) Others were creepy, like the small spiders that crawled out from under the wall where the baseboard molding should have been, and the large one that hung suspended above my son's bed, only to disappear into a hole in the ceiling if anyone tried to get it. Still other issues were far more serious. It began to feel overwhelming, and with the news of each problem, I'd get a pit in my stomach. I think of depression and anxiety as siblings, and by this time they had both moved in.

One day, just after the electrician left, I turned on the light switch in our bedroom—and the light in the bathroom went out! Our daughter, who was taking a bath, was left shrieking in the dark. That's the day I decided that the house didn't like me any more than I liked it. My prayer became, quite simply, "God, get me out of here!"

My participation in a Bible study continued, but I found that words—even God's word—did not always resonate in my foggy mind. However, the hugs and smiles from my group showed their care and helped me feel God's love. I called this "hug theology."

Little did I know that soon God would choose another nonverbal way to communicate with me.

I brought up the idea of moving again, but my husband felt that could spell financial disaster. So, I became determined to make the place feel like ours by hanging pictures and starting the remodel. (It seems that sometimes after we quit our bitter complaining and reach some level of acceptance, then we see God is at work.)

Not long afterwards, I walked to the mailbox and found a note inside. It began: "Hello. We are the family that was in line to buy the home you just purchased . . . " It stated they had not found a home to meet their needs, and if we ever wanted to sell, they were still interested. *Wait. Did I read that right?* I read it again. During the years my mother worked as a realtor, I had heard some unusual stories, but never anything like this. *The family still wanted this place?! Could it be that God was offering us a way out?*

I responded to the note with a phone call. I got the impression they had a more generous remodeling budget than we did. However, they didn't want to sound too anxious to buy the house, and I tried not to show how desperately I wanted to sell it, so the conversation was inconclusive. I hung up and turned toward the window. There, arching over the lake, was the most beautiful, bright rainbow I had ever seen. It was stunning! Wordlessly, it spoke to my heart. I was not forgotten. There was hope.

> Whenever I bring clouds over the earth and the rainbow appears in the clouds, I will remember my covenant between me and you and all living creatures of every kind. Never again will the waters become a flood to destroy all life (Gen 9:14–15).

The rainbow is a sign of God's promise, and I told my daughter this particular rainbow was God's promise our home would no longer be flooded with tears.

What would happen next, I didn't know, but I did know God was with us. I wondered if just the awareness that someone else was interested in the place would help me be more appreciative of it. A few days later, a Purchase and Sale agreement, signed by the interested family, was dropped on our front porch. They were serious, and this was a good offer. We negotiated an agreement, to be finalized when we found another home. There were boxes that hadn't even been unpacked yet. Wouldn't that make moving easier?

We began looking at homes once more. I happened to drive by an open house one day. Later, my husband and I both popped in and loved it, however, it was a little too pricey for us. Then the price dropped significantly. Perfect! An appointment was set with the realtor, but it was snatched up before we arrived. My heart sank. Later that day, as I was picking my kids up from school, I saw another rainbow. It gave me hope that God had something better for us.

Finally, we found a property that seemed right. It was pretty, with a homey feel that reminded us of our first house in the trees. Best of all, the lot had an open southern exposure. In fact, this house would get better light than the one we had recently missed out on. We were now focused on the home itself, rather than a lake view, but I got a kick out of the fact that it happened to be across the street from a large pond. Our realtor said he thought it would sell quickly, a comment he'd never made about another place.

Finding a home we liked was good news for us, and also for the people who wanted our lakeview house. I quickly called to tell that family. No answer. I left messages, but they didn't call back. The circumstances were such that we needed them to finalize that sale or our family would risk being stuck with two mortgages. I knew my husband would never be comfortable taking such a chance, and it was important for me to honor his feelings. I prayed, "Lord, if that is to be our home, please hold it for us!" Realizing the schools were on spring break, I began to suspect the interested family was on vacation. This was before everyone carried a cell phone, so all we could do was wait and pray.

A few days later, I took my two kids and another child to see the Tigger movie, in which Tigger is looking for his family home. I could relate—so much so that I was fighting back tears. It was a little embarrassing to be the only person—certainly the only adult—crying at the Tigger movie. Driving back, as we came up the hill from the lake, my son said "Look, Mom! A rainbow!" Now let me pause here for a moment. Yes, it rains a lot in this area. Occasionally, the sun comes out and a rainbow can be seen. But that's more common in the spring and it was still winter. And this was now the third rainbow I'd seen at a significant point in my journey. It did not feel like coincidence. On that particular afternoon, I felt God had seen my tears and was reminding me to put my hope in him.

The wait seemed interminable, but the other family finally returned from vacation. The very next day, they purchased the old lakeview house with no contingencies, allowing us to purchase our next home. We moved again.

My doctor helped me find a medicine that rebalanced my brain chemistry and lifted the fog of depression, and I continued to heal in our new residence. As we were settling in, my son and I took a walk to get acquainted with our neighborhood. Turning back toward our home by the pond, we saw a bright rainbow curving over it. God had been faithful to his promises and had brought us through the storm. Psalm 50:14–15 seemed to sum up my experience:

> Offer to God a sacrifice of thanksgiving, and pay your vows to
> the Most High;
> and call upon me in the day of trouble; I will deliver you and
> you shall glorify me.

God had delivered me. It was time to praise him and move into the future he had waiting for me.

It is still important for me to be intentional about my physical and mental health, especially as winter approaches, but on those days that my old foes come calling, I try to remember:

1. I am not alone.

2. It won't last forever.

3. God is true to his promises.

Loving Father,
Thank you for your promise to never abandon us,
even in a mess that is largely of our own making. Amen.

CHAPTER 17—DIVING DEEPER

REFLECT

1. Have you experienced assurance of God's presence during a difficult time? How was that communicated to you?

2. Through most of my dark days, I didn't feel like smiling. Do you think there is an expectation that people of faith wear a smile at all times? Is this appropriate?

3. In addition to the rainbow after the great flood in Genesis, we also read about rainbows in John's visions in Revelation. Describing heaven's throne, John writes, "A rainbow, resembling an emerald, encircled the throne" (Rev 4:3b). Later, John has a vision of a mighty angel, and writes "He was robed in a cloud, with a rainbow above his head; and his face was like the sun" (Rev 10:1). What do you think these rainbows signify? What do they tell you about God?

GIVE THANKS

- for God's promise to always be with us.

- for friends and family who stand by us when the going gets rough, and give comforting hugs or other signs of reassurance.

- for the myriad ways God uses his creation to speak to our hearts.

READ

The LORD makes firm the steps of the one who delights in him; though he may stumble, he will not fall, for the LORD upholds him with his hand (Ps 37:23–24).

Pss 23, 40, 42, 43—King David's honesty before God

Josh 1:9—God will be with us wherever we go

Isa 49:14–16—engraved on the palms of God's hands

John 1:5—The light shines in the darkness

ACT

Do you know someone who has seemed down lately? Choose one of these ways to show your support:

- Call or write a note.
- Invite that person to take a walk or hike with you out in nature.
- Give nonverbal support: a reassuring smile or touch, a small gift, cheerful flowers, etc.

If you are the one who is feeling down, do something nice for yourself. Take a walk, call a friend, treat yourself to flowers . . . and don't be afraid to reach out for support.

Chapter 18

GATHERING TREASURES

Where there is ruin, there is hope for a treasure.

RUMI

Do you enjoy walking along the beach, seeing what treasures the waves have left behind? Depending on the location, you may find smooth stones, driftwood, sand dollars, or a variety of shells. One of my favorite things to look for is sea glass. Often, a colorful piece finds its way home with me and ends up in a jar on my windowsill. When I found three pieces—clear, light blue, and cobalt— I fashioned them into a necklace.

Sometimes, as I hold a piece of beach glass in my hand, I wonder about its history. It only offers hints of what it once was. Most often, it was part of a bottle. Perhaps it held a soft drink, expensive perfume—or someone's beer. Sea glass is particularly abundant at certain beaches, such as at Glass Beach in Fort Bragg, California, where trash was thrown from the cliff above. Regardless of what the glass was originally a part of, it got shattered. Afterwards, the jagged pieces no longer served their original purpose. They continued to be dashed against the rocks, tumbled in the waves, and pounded into the sand again and again. Through this long and torturous process, the broken pieces were gradually transformed until the edges were smoothed and the surface took on the look of frosted glass. What was once simply refuse became something beautiful, even cherished.

Just as the sea tumbles beach glass until it becomes a thing of beauty, so God can take the broken pieces of our lives and transform them. Our God not only has the ability to create, but also to restore, redeem, renew, and even resurrect. After all, this is the God who said, "Behold, I will do a new thing; now it shall spring forth; shall ye not know it? I will even make a way in the wilderness, *and* rivers in the desert" (Isa 43:19 KJV). And in case we missed that, Revelation 21:5 states, "Behold, I make all things new" (KJV).

People who really love beachcombing know that the best time to go is following rough weather, when big waves have washed both trash and treasure ashore. After a storm has passed through our lives, we may find items of meaning and beauty amid the rubble, too. Some experiences we go through are awful and evil, grieving our hearts and the heart of God. Yet, no matter how heart-wrenching the situation is, Scripture assures us that God still loves us, is with us in the midst of it, and is at work to bring something good from it. Even without being grateful for the storm itself, we may thankfully acknowledge the treasures we have found.

If we look, we often find we are left with gifts of wisdom and empathy. Years ago, I was in a difficult situation, but had a sense there was something of value to be learned. I remember praying, *Lord, I don't like this! But as long as I'm here, let me stay just long enough to learn something. (Then, please get me out quickly!)*

When we are in the middle of a situation, we can't see the whole picture, but as we look back later, we may gain perspective. Sometimes things are clearer in the rear-view mirror. Even then, we aren't always aware that any good that came from a rough time, but I do love the times we see it clearly.

A relative of mine shared this story: As a young attorney, his disagreeable boss created a toxic work environment. If you've ever had to face a prickly employer day after day, you know how tough that is. However, I suspect he'd do it all again because, while that job is now a distant memory, he recently celebrated his 50th anniversary with the charming woman he met there. For him, an unpleasant situation held a delightful surprise he never imagined.

We all have times when illness or injury stands in the way of what we want to do. Years ago, a friend told me he was supposed to go on an important business trip, but he got sick and had to cancel. Had he gone, he might never have returned. His itinerary had included meetings at the World Trade Center in New York, on September 11, 2001.

What we think is an ending may turn out to be an important beginning. There was a woman who had done farm work all her life, and liked working, but found it too difficult as she got older. In order to fill her time, she took up embroidery—until arthritis forced her to give *that* up. Sounds to me like a one-two punch. How frustrating! She returned to an activity she had enjoyed in her younger years—painting—and two years later, an art collector discovered her work. The artist's name was Anna Mary Robertson Moses—Grandma Moses. Had she continued to work on the farm or occupied herself with embroidery, the world might never have known the joyful paintings she became famous for.

We find another striking example in the story of Joseph. As a young man, he endured the trauma of being thrown into a pit by his brothers and then sold into slavery in Egypt. It was certainly not the most pleasant way to end up in another country, but God had great plans for him there! He missed the famine in his home-land of Canaan, and ended up in a position of such power that he was able to provide for the citizens of his new country, as well as save his whole family from starvation. When Joseph was finally reconciled with his brothers, he told them, "You intended to harm me, but God intended it for good to accomplish what is now being done, the saving of many lives" (Gen 50:20).

Low points in life can prove to be productive times. For example, the apostle Paul wrote amazing letters from prison. King David wrote heartfelt psalms during the years he spent hiding in caves. What a treasure these writings are!

Jesus' death gives us the ultimate example of something positive coming out of a horrible situation. I used to wonder why the day he died is called "Good Friday." What could possibly be good about the crucifixion of an innocent man? And yet—somehow all this was for our good. As Isaiah says, "by his stripes we are healed" (Isa 53:5). Not only was his death for our benefit, but only those who have died can be resurrected. By his resurrection, Jesus defeated death itself.

We began this chapter thinking about beach glass. There is another type of glass that also illustrates beauty emerging from destruction. I live in Washington, home to Mt. St. Helens, infamous for its explosive 1980 eruption. The destructive power of the blast was mind-boggling! I remember a relative recounting her experience in the eastern part of the state. Although hundreds of miles away, the wind was blowing so much ash that direction that daytime seemed like night and the streetlights came on in mid-afternoon. Now, a stone made from that ash is used as a gemstone in jewelry. It is called helenite, or Mount St. Helens obsidian. Green is the most common color, resembling an emerald. To me, this is a literal picture of "beauty instead of ashes"— words that are found in Isaiah's prophetic vision, which Jesus read from as he began his ministry.

> The Spirit of the Sovereign LORD is on me,
> because the LORD has anointed me to proclaim good news to
> the poor.
> He has sent me to bind up the brokenhearted,
> to proclaim freedom for the captives and release from darkness
> for the prisoners,
> to proclaim the year of the LORD's favor and the day of ven-
> geance of our God,
> to comfort all who mourn and provide for those who grieve in
> Zion—
> to bestow on them a crown of beauty instead of ashes,
> the oil of joy instead of mourning,
> and a garment of praise instead of a spirit of despair.
> They will be called oaks of righteousness,
> a planting of the LORD for the display of his splendor.
> (Isa 61:1–3; see also Luke 4:18–19)

Dear Lord,
Where we see nothing but destruction, you see opportunity.
Thank you that you are a God of second chances, a God of
redemption, a creative God who makes all things new.
Help us remember that nothing we face can ever separate us
from your love or thwart your purpose for us.
Amen.

CHAPTER 18—DIVING DEEPER

REFLECT

1. Can you think of a time when your plans were foiled—and it worked out for the best?

2. Have you ever had a miserable experience that ended up providing important clarity for your future?

3. Do you know someone who has dealt with a challenging situation, and now works passionately to help those who are going through similar difficulties?

GIVE THANKS

Offer thanks for the gifts you have gained through tough times, such as:

- wisdom

- empathy

- closer relationships, and awareness of how much people care for you

- a sense of God's presence

Are there other gifts you would add?

Think of a present struggle you would like to be free from. Can you see any possibility of something good coming out of the experience? Offer thanks that God is at work, even when you don't see it.

READ

> And we know that in all things God works for the good
> of those who love him, who have been called according
> to his purpose. (Rom 8:28)

(Please allow me to make a comment here, as I often hear this verse used in a way that I don't think Paul intended. Previously, when we looked at 1 Thessalonians 5:18, we noted that Paul's instructions were "give thanks *in* all circumstances," not necessarily *for* all circumstances. In a similar way, here Paul writes that God can bring good *from* all things. He does not say all things *are*, in themselves, good.)

Joel 2:25—restoration

Isa 54:1–5—rejoicing after suffering

Rom 8:38—nothing can separate us from the love of God.

ACT

Is there a way you can use your own difficult experience in order to help others this week?

Next time you are fighting the wind and the waves—and afterward—keep your eyes open for treasures. If you keep a journal, make note of them.

Part IV

Built on a Rock

Chapter 19

Swim Cover-Up

I delight greatly in the LORD;
My soul rejoices in my God.
For he has clothed me with garments of salvation
and arrayed me in a robe of righteousness.

ISAIAH 61:10

RECENTLY, MY SISTER-IN-LAW WAS visiting and joined us for some fun on a nearby lake. Later that day, we met again for a family dinner. She was wearing a cute, simple dress. But it wasn't really a dress. It was a swim cover-up.

When we put on our swimsuits and head for the beach, we often grab a cover-up. We don't want too much skin exposed to the sun. For men, a T-shirt may be enough. For women, it can get more complicated. Not only do we want sun protection, we also don't want every lump and bump, stretch mark, or spider vein in full view. Even when we exercise and eat right, most of us do not look quite like the perfect, air-brushed images we see in magazines, and may be hyper-aware of anything we consider to be a flaw. A cover-up can help us feel less self-conscious.

There is a spiritual equivalent to the beach cover-up. Just as the bright summer sun exposes our physical imperfections, so standing in God's light clearly reveals the shortcomings of our souls. Psalm 90, which is attributed to Moses, reads, "You have set our iniquities before you, our secret sins in the light of your presence" (v. 8). And Paul noted, "everything exposed by the light becomes visible" (Eph 5:13a).

If we honestly examine our hearts, our motives, and our thoughts, we have to admit we don't always like what we see. And that doesn't include the faults we are blind to! The idea of being fully exposed in God's light can leave us feeling naked, caught like a deer in the headlights. As wise King Solomon observed, "Who can say 'I have kept my heart pure; I am clean and without sin'?" (Prov 20:9). Some people try to feel better by comparing themselves favorably to others. But that won't make them more perfect—only smugger. Others think they just need to work hard at being a good person and obeying God's laws. But the truth is, no matter how hard we try, none of us can ever be wholly holy!

But here's where God steps in. Our Creator wants us to be with him and has provided a way by which our shortcomings can be forgiven and covered. This allows us to stand freely in his light. I can't begin to explain all the mysteries of God's kingdom, but there is one thing I am certain of: the only way any of us can stand in God's presence is by the gift of God's grace. This grace is offered to all, and it is up to us to accept the gift and welcome God's presence into our lives.

Did you know our gracious God has been providing cover-ups for mankind since the beginning? Let's check in on Adam and Eve. We find them in the garden God lovingly created for them. Regrettably, they were not content to simply be God's beloved children, under his care and guidance. They wanted more, and did the one thing they were instructed not to do. Immediately, this put a palpable distance between them and their Creator. They had been walking innocently with God. Now they felt so awkward they hid from him. They attempted to cover themselves by sewing together fig leaves. Think of that for a moment. If those leaf-clothes didn't tear the first hour, they'd surely be crumbling in a few days. In his great compassion, God made more durable clothes for them—garments of animal skins (Gen 3:21).

Presumably Adam and Eve's new outfits came at the cost of the life of a newly formed creature. Later, every time God's chosen people offered an animal sacrifice at the temple, or sent a scapegoat into the wilderness, they were reminded of the seriousness of not living up to their calling, and the cost of forgiveness.

When John the Baptist saw Jesus, he introduced him as "the Lamb of God, who takes away the sin of the world" (John 1:29), referencing both the temple sacrifices and the Passover lamb. In the dramatic account of God's rescue of the Israelites from slavery in Egypt, the people were instructed to slaughter a lamb, dip a branch in the blood, and paint it onto the top and both sides of the doorframe. This was a sign of divine protection. Judgment fell on the land of Egypt, but *passed over* those homes.

Although Jesus was innocent, he carried our offenses to his execution so we could wear his righteousness. In his role as priest, Jesus did more than just offer a sacrifice—he *was* the sacrifice. When we trust in him, we are marked as God's own. We are forgiven. Then, when God the Father looks at us, he sees the righteousness of Jesus, as though Jesus has wrapped his own priestly robe protectively around us.

The Hebrew word usually translated "salvation" encompasses the physical as well as the spiritual. It means "save, rescue, deliver, help, preserve, give victory." Jesus's very name—*Yeshua*, in Hebrew—is closely related to that word and means "the Lord is salvation." Likewise, the Greek word *sozo*, usually translated as "save," contains a much fuller meaning than our English word, including "rescue, deliver, and *heal*." I love this because we are so much more than our mistakes, and God works with us to become everything we were designed to be. God wants wholeness for us—wholeness for our bodies, souls, and relationships.

When we act in opposition to God's loving instruction, relationships fracture in all directions. For example, Adam and Eve's act of defiance not only distanced them from their Creator, but also strained the relationship between the two of them. Our shortcomings affect each of us internally, as well, and can make it uncomfortable to face ourselves in the mirror. Thankfully, our loving God does more than throw the robe of righteousness at us and tell us to cover up. God forgives us, asks us to turn from those things that are harming us, and helps us move toward a more fulfilling way of life. It's like someone who hears a good friend say they want to lose weight and responds, "I love you no matter what you weigh. Even so, I want to support you in your pursuit of a healthier lifestyle. Let me come alongside. I'd love to go to the gym with you or take a walk together." As we considered in the last chapter, God not only creates, but also wants to restore, redeem, renew, and even resurrect.

As we wrap up this chapter, let's look at one of my favorite passages from the same book we started with, the book of the prophet Isaiah. To me, it clearly illustrates the workings of God's kingdom—with a water theme (of course). As you read, pay particular attention to the order. Isaiah says it so beautifully, and it all begins with God!

> You heavens above, rain down my righteousness;
> Let the clouds shower it down.
> Let the earth open wide,
> Let salvation spring up,
> Let righteousness flourish with it;
> I, the LORD, have created it (Isa 45:8).

- ↝ God rains down righteousness

- ↝ The earth opens to accept it

- ↝ Salvation ensues

- ↝ Righteousness flourishes

I can't think of a more fitting way to end this chapter than with the words of the psalmist:

> Come, let us sing for joy to the LORD;
> Let us shout aloud to the Rock of our salvation (Ps 95:1).

Lord God,
The words "thank you" are so inadequate. You bless our planet
and our crops with rain. In your grace, you offer your people
cleansing, forgiveness, and garments of salvation. You save,
rescue, deliver, and heal. Help us accept your astounding gifts
with gratitude and learn to walk, unafraid, in your light.
In the name of Jesus (Yeshua), our Messiah,
Amen.

CHAPTER 19—DIVING DEEPER

REFLECT

1. When you think of the robe of righteousness, does a visual image come to mind? If so, try to describe it. Are there passages in the Bible that suggest what it might look like?

2. Just as God offers us grace and forgiveness, he asks us to extend the same to others. Are you holding onto resentment and need to begin the process of forgiving someone?

3. Do you have a favorite quote or saying (from the Bible or elsewhere) that illuminates your understanding of the workings of God's kingdom? How does it speak to you?

GIVE THANKS

~ for God's provision of a clean, white robe.

~ for Jesus' sacrifice.

~ for the Spirit's help to live restored and free of shame.

READ

For it is by grace you have been saved, through faith—and this is not from yourselves, it is the gift of God—not by works, so that no one can boast (Eph 2:8–9).

1 John 1:8–9—confession, forgiveness, and cleansing

Rom 3:21–24—righteousness from God through faith

2 Cor 5:21—trade sin for righteousness

Gal 3:26–27—clothed with Christ

Rev 16:15—stay awake and clothed!

ACT

Ask for the Spirit's help in examining your heart to determine areas in which you have shortcomings. Confess these, then ask for God's help to strengthen you as you turn and move in a new direction.

If you identified someone in the second Reflection question, take a step toward forgiveness and, if appropriate, let that person know they are forgiven.

Chapter 20

LIGHTHOUSE

You're here to be light,
bringing out the God-colors in the world.

MATTHEW 5:14A (MSG)

WHETHER SEEN FROM LAND or from aboard a ship, many people love the sight of a lighthouse. It is a symbol of hope, strength, safety, and protection. For people of faith, it can be a reminder that, no matter how difficult the journey, God is there to help guide us home.

Lighthouses in the United States are automated now, with only one exception (Boston Light, in the Boston Harbor Islands National Recreation Area). Even so, for those of us who love the water, it's easy to fantasize about what it would have been like to live in one and be the lightkeeper. Many of the keepers dearly loved their work, but it was not easy. Keeping the beacons lit and fog signals functioning was a heavy responsibility. It was often lonely work, too, as many locations were isolated, and some were only accessible by boat.

Daily tasks included lighting the lamp each evening, trimming the wick at midnight, and putting it out in the morning. Each of these required a trip up and down a winding staircase in the tower. In some locales, this is equivalent to climbing to the top floor of a twelve-story building—or even higher. If the fog signal wasn't working, some keepers needed to walk out on a long dock to ring a fog bell at regular intervals. When a shipwreck occurred nearby, the lightkeeper often became a rescue crew of one. During inclement weather, everything became exponentially more difficult.

Lighthouses can be seen on cliffs overlooking the ocean and on various waterways, such as the Great Lakes and New York Harbor. It's crucial that a ship's captain be able to clearly identify which lighthouse is which. Therefore, no two look quite the same, or shine their light in the exact same way. By day, a lighthouse can be recognized by its unique colors and paint design, known as a daymark. A distinctive series of flashes serves to identify the light at night. This is known as known as the daytime or nighttime characteristic.

Like beacons, God's people are called to be lights in the darkness. In the last chapter, we looked at a short quote from Ephesians 5:13: "everything exposed by the light becomes visible." Paul's next words were, "and everything that is illuminated becomes a light." When God's word shines in our hearts, we reflect God's brightness out into the world, with each person reflecting God's light in a unique way. Whoever you are and wherever you find yourself, the world needs *your* light!

Lighthouses are most helpful to ships when they can be seen from far out to sea. In the early 1800s, a new type of lens was developed by the French physicist Augustin-Jean Fresnel. It allowed a light to be seen from further away than ever before, and became known as "the invention that saved a million ships." The Fresnel lens uses the principles of refraction, focus, and magnification. I find it fascinating that the same words apply to our own ability to shine. Refraction has to do with a change of direction, bending a beam of light. As discussed in the last chapter, we all need to turn and change direction at times. Then, we focus our energy in a more constructive way, possibly on an area of service we are called to. Finally, we come to magnification. One definition of this word is "to praise or glorify." We do not shine to bring glory to ourselves, but to God. As David wrote, "O magnify the LORD with me, and let us exalt his name together!" (Ps 34:3 ESV).

While the lightkeepers did their best to keep people safe, there were others who had the opposite goal in mind. In times of war, lightkeepers were sometimes threatened. For instance, during the American Revolution, the British tried to prevent them from doing their jobs in order to disrupt the Colonists' trade. Even in peacetime, greedy people could benefit from looting ships. It was not unheard of for these exploiters to stand on shore holding a light to deceive ships' captains into thinking that was the lighthouse, and thus lure ships straight onto the rocks.

We, too, have an enemy who wants to prevent us from shining God's light into the lives of others. Much like those cruel people holding lanterns to confuse captains and cause shipwrecks, we read that our enemy sometimes masquerades as an "angel of light" (2 Cor 11:14). In order to stand firm, our lives must be firmly grounded in God, our Rock. Jesus stressed the importance of firm footing when he told a parable contrasting building a house on solid rock versus on the sand (Matt 7:24–25). Lighthouses are typically built on high, rocky ground, not on the sand where the tide would wash the foundation out from under it.

In reading about the life of lightkeepers, I noticed they spent a lot of time cleaning. In particular, they were constantly polishing the lens and the lantern, and washing the windows of the lantern room. This wasn't just because they were clean freaks. They worked hard to keep the light burning, and didn't want it dimmed by dirty glass. They wanted it to shine as brightly as possible.

Some days we may feel like God's light is a bonfire in our hearts. Other days it may seem more like a smoldering wick. Either way, by providing optimum conditions for God's love and light to shine through us, we can help illuminate the way for others.

I invite you to partner with me for these last few pages. Before closing this book, I would encourage you to flip through it once more. Were there topics that particularly spoke to you or ideas that you would like to incorporate into your life? Were there beach bag items you want to carry more consistently, or activities you wish to remove in order to make room for something of greater value? These questions may point to ways you can let the light shine more clearly.

Please don't worry that this is a call to push yourself harder, to do more, be more, or add one more unnecessary thing to your schedule. You may even look back through these chapters and realize that focusing on the "Beach Chair" (ch. 8) would be most helpful to you. Maybe the most life-giving thing you can do right now is build more rest into your life so you can be at your loving, patient best with your family and/or coworkers.

Perhaps chapter 2, "Beach Creatures," whispered to a deep insecurity. It could be that what you most need to take away from this book is to remember that you are a unique creation of God, beloved and wonderful, even in your imperfection.

Once you identify a helpful direction, it's go time. You have probably heard the quote from Lao Tzu, "A thousand-mile journey begins with a single step."* Actually, I've read that a more accurate translation is "The journey of a thousand miles begins beneath one's feet." I love that! You start right where you already are, with the resources you already have. And you know what? If you're standing on The Rock, you have an excellent starting place.

You may be thinking, "You're talking about a journey and I haven't even figured out which direction to head!" In that case, a good first step would be to set aside dedicated time to ponder, pray, and journal in order to discern what would be most beneficial to you.

When I think of first steps, it always brings to mind a scene from one of my favorite movies, *What About Bob?*, starring Bill Murray as Bob. The poor guy suffers from all sorts of severe phobias and his psychiatrist tries to help him, using the principle of "baby steps." Bob enthusiastically embraces this idea. Although just being out in public is unnerving for him, he gingerly walks out of the psychiatrist's office, repeating the words "baby steps, baby steps" to himself. Then, "baby steps down the hall." Finally,

---

* Tzu, *Tao Te Ching*, 64.

"baby steps into the elevator." Everything is going so well—until the elevator descends and we hear Bob's scream echo through the shaft! Guess he wasn't quite ready for that yet. But he did make progress. This idea of baby steps is important. Great achievements begin with small steps. I suggest:

- Be specific, so you know what it is you're going to do and when it's completed.
- Set a time frame and DO it.

It helps to write each planned step down, mark it on your calendar, and tell at least one person. You might even invite someone in your study group, a friend, or family member to be your accountability partner. Once you have taken the first step, you're on your way and the following steps become easier. It may take a lot of work to polish an enormous lens, but it's easy to buff up one spot, followed by another.

In closing, I want to say it has been an honor to travel through this book—and along the beach—with you. My friend Jenny, who graced these pages with her artwork, commented that when people have been to the beach, it's easy to tell. They have a sunny glow on their faces and a relaxation about them.

God of light,
May we spend sufficient time in your presence that those
around us can catch a glimpse of your radiance in our faces,
your peace in our hearts, and your love in our care for all
creation. So be it (Amen).

CHAPTER 20—DIVING DEEPER

REFLECT

John declares: "God is light; in him there is no darkness at all" (1 John 1:5).

1. What does it mean that "God is light?"

2. How does God's light shine on you?

3. How does God's light shine through you?

4. Are there attitudes, activities, or preoccupations that act as "dirty windows," dulling the brightness of the light?

GIVE THANKS

- that you are loved just the way you are.

- for the light of God's word that shines on your path.

- that you have the privilege of reflecting God's light to others.

READ

Here's another way to put it: You're here to be light, bringing out the God-colors in the world. God is not a secret to be kept. We're going public with this, as public as a city on a hill. If I make you light-bearers, you don't think I'm going to hide you under a bucket, do you? I'm putting you on a light stand. Now that I've put you there on a hilltop, on a light stand—shine! (Matt 5:14–16 MSG)

Ps 27:1—"The LORD is my light and my salvation . . .."

Ps 36:9—life and light

2 Cor 4:5–6—God's light in our hearts

1 Sam 2:2; Pss 18:31; 40:2—God is our Rock

ACT

Did question 4 in the Reflect section lead you to discover some "dirty windows?" Get the smudges out!

If there was a chapter or section of this book that particularly spoke to you, reread it and try to discern a helpful action step for your life.

Did a passage of Scripture grab your attention? Dig into it, memorize it, live it.

If you have been reading this book in a study group, discuss whether some or all of the members would like to meet again to share first steps, and even continue meeting (perhaps every other week or monthly) to encourage each other along your chosen paths.

Send me your light and your faithful care,
let them lead me;
Let them bring me to your holy mountain,
to the place where you dwell.

PSALM 43:3

Suggested Resources

Chapter 1: Water

"Sea Fever," *Salt-Water Ballads,* by John Masefield.

Blue Mind: The Surprising Science That Shows How Being Near, in, on, or Underwater Can Make You Happier, Healthier, More Connected, and Better at What You Do by Wallace J. Nichols

Henry and Mudge and the Forever Sea by Cynthia Rylant. You and any little ones in your life will feel like you're enjoying a day at the seaside with young Henry, his dad, and his big dog, Mudge.

Chapter 2: Beach Creatures

Abba's Child by Brennan Manning

The Gifts of Imperfection: Let Go of Who You Think You're Supposed to Be and Embrace Who You Are by Brene Brown

Chapter 3: Bring a Friend

The Five Love Languages by Gary Chapman. Since it was first written, various versions have been published.

Chapter 4: Community

A Year of Living Kindly by Donna Cameron

Chapter 5: Sunglasses

Pollyanna by Eleanor Porter. Although "Pollyanna" has come to mean someone who is annoyingly optimistic, I suspect this has a lot to do with the character's portrayal in the Disney movie. I think it's worth giving this 1913 classic book a chance.

Chapter 6: Flip-Flops

Gift from the Sea by Anne Morrow Lindbergh. This book is a delight!

How to Live in Flip-Flops by Sandy Gingras. This is a fun, light-hearted little book.

100 Ways to Simplify Your Life by Joyce Meyer

Chapter 7: What Are You Carrying?

The Best Yes: Making Wise Decisions in the Midst of Endless Demands by Lysa TerKeurst. In this book, Lysa offers suggestions for gently saying "no."

Having a Mary Heart in a Martha World: Finding Intimacy with God in the Busyness of Life by Joanna Weaver. I highly recommend this title.

Taming the To-Do List: How to Choose Your Best Work Every Day by Glynnis Whitwer

Chapter 8: Beach Chair

See *Having a Mary Heart in a Martha World*, listed under resources for chapter 7.

Chapter 9: Life Ring

Before Amen by Max Lucado

Draw the Circle: The 40-Day Prayer Challenge by Mark Batterson

How Strong Women Pray by Bonnie St. John. Along with her own stories, Bonnie features interviews with a variety of strong women.

Walking with God by John Eldredge

Chapter 10: Lip Balm

The Boy, the Mole, the Fox and the Horse by Charlie Mackesy. This charming little book contains great wisdom.

Chapter 11: Good Book

Reading the Bible with Rabbi Jesus: How a Jewish Perspective Can Transform Your Understanding by Lois Tverberg

Sitting at the Feet of Rabbi Jesus: How the Jewishness of Jesus Can Transform your Faith by Ann Spangler and Lois Tverberg

Word Study Bibles and Key Word Study Bibles have an English text, but allow the reader to look up the exact meaning of the original Greek or Hebrew.

Apps—Here are just a few to check out:

Bible Hub is like having a reference library on your phone.

NIV Bible (New International Version) makes it so easy to look up a reference.

Olive Tree Bible

Websites:
NETbible.org (New English Translation). It'll even read to you!

BibleGateway.com

Use your favorite web search engine to find a phrase or reference.

Chapter 12: Beach Ball

The Art of the Possible by Alexandra Stoddard

The Book of JOY by His Holiness the Dalai Lama and Archbishop Desmond Tutu, with Douglas Abrams.

Live Your Joy by Bonnie St. John

One Thousand Gifts byAnn Voskamp

Chapter 13: Into the Storm

Heaven Is Real: Lessons on Earthly Joy—From the Man Who Spent 90 Minutes in Heaven by Don Piper

It's Not Supposed to Be This Way by Lysa TerKeurst

A Shepherd Looks at Psalm 23 by Phillip Keller

When Life Gives You Pears: The Healing Power of Family, Faith, and Funny People by Jeannie Gaffigan. Who else could find the humor in a brain tumor?

Chapter 14: A Stowaway in the Bag

Having a Mary Heart in a Martha World, listed under resources for chapter 7, also addresses fear and worry.

The Lord Is My Shepherd by Harold S. Kushner

Chapter 15: The Waves of Doubt

If I Really Believe, Why Do I Have These Doubts? by Dr. Lynn Anderson

Chapter 16: Boundaries

Boundaries: When to Say Yes, How to Say No to Take Control of Your Life by Henry Cloud and John Townsend. Other titles include *Boundaries in Marriage.*

Codependent No More: How to Stop Controlling Others and Start Caring for Yourself by Melody Beattie. Helpful for those struggling with true codependency.

Website: LeslieVernick.com. Leslie is a Christian counselor offering support for people in destructive relationships.

Chapter 17: Out of the Darkness

In the Middle of the Mess: Strength for This Beautiful, Broken Life by Sheila Walsh

Chapter 18: Gathering Treasures

He Speaks in the Silence: Finding Intimacy with God by Learning to Listen by Diane Comer. Diane tells of learning to hear God after going deaf.

"KaBoom." Post on my website: Splashes of Encouragement (Splashesofencouragement.com). Click "blog" at the top and keep scrolling down to 9/7/2019.

Chapter 19: Swimsuit Cover-up

Abba's Child by Brennan Manning

Chapter 20: Lighthouse

Rhythms of Renewal: Trading Stress and Anxiety for a Life of Peace and Purpose by Rebekah Lyons

Women Who Kept the Lights: An Illustrated History of Female Lighthouse Keepers by Mary Louise Clifford and J. Candace Clifford. Glimpses into the lives of women lighthouse keepers spanning the years from 1776 to 1947, with journal entries and historical photos.

You Are the Girl for the Job: Daring to Believe the God Who Calls You by Jess Connolly

Bibliography

Drummond, Henry. *The Greatest Thing in the World and Other Addresses*. New York: Revell, 1891.

The History Hour. *The Entire Life Story of Franklin Delano Roosevelt: Conquering Fear*. Great Biographies 12. s.l.: The History Hour, 2018.

Longfellow, Henry Wadsworth. *The Complete Poetical Works of Henry Wadsworth Longfellow*. Boston: Houghton Mifflin, 1922.

Spurgeon, Charles H. *Morning & Evening*. Grand Rapids: Zondervan, 1980.

Tzu, Lao. *Tao Te Ching*. Translated by Stephen Addiss and Stanley Lombardo. Indianapolis, IN: Hackett, 1993.

Made in the USA
Las Vegas, NV
16 March 2023

69204733R00115